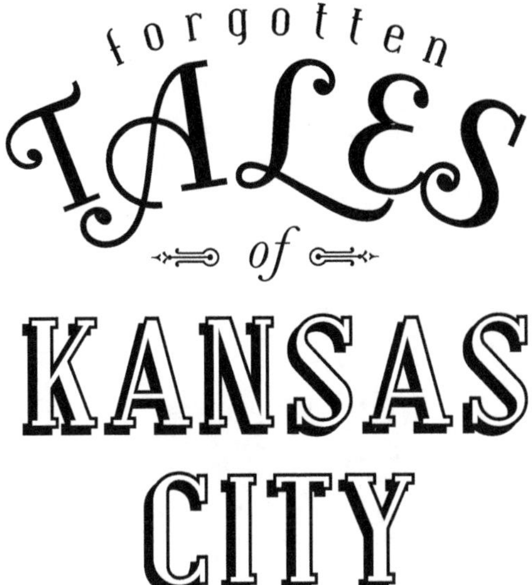
forgotten
TALES
of
KANSAS
CITY

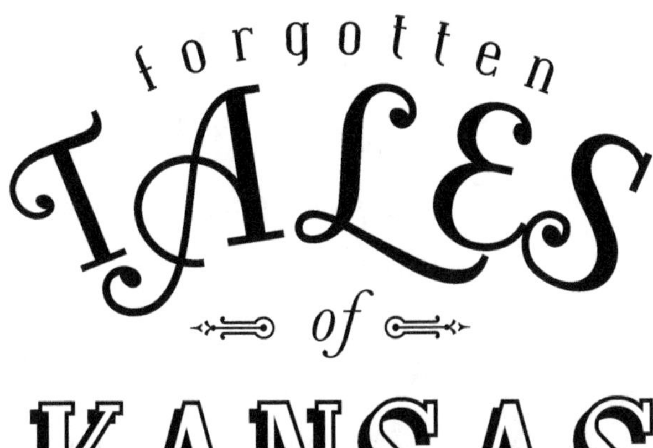

Forgotten Tales of Kansas City

Paul Kirkman

illustrations by

Kristen Solecki

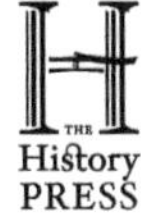

The History Press

Published by The History Press
Charleston, SC 29403
www.historypress.net

Illustrations by Kristen Solecki

First published 2012

ISBN 978-1-5402-0703-6

Library of Congress Cataloging-in-Publication Data

Kirkman, Paul.
Forgotten tales of Kansas City / Paul Kirkman.
pages cm
Includes bibliographical references.
ISBN 978-1-5402-0703-6
1. Kansas City (Mo.)--History--Anecdotes. 2. Kansas City (Mo.)--Biography--Anecdotes. I. Title.
F474.K257K47 2012
977.8'411--dc23
2012039305

Notice: The information in this book is true and complete to the best of our knowledge. It is offered without guarantee on the part of the author or The History Press. The author and The History Press disclaim all liability in connection with the use of this book.

Preface

In the 1800s, the "easy" way west ended at Missouri's western border, the political boundary of the United States until 1854. The Missouri River turns north near the mouth of the Kaw, and travelers had to go overland from that point on. The hard way, the long ride—or, more often, the long walk beside a wagon—started here.

Expansion hesitated at the Missouri line. People paused at the edge of the prairie, where water, trees and safety became sparse. Uncertainty, deserts, mountains and untamed land spread before the traveler. Wild beasts and wilder men inhabited the land between the trail's head and the trail's end. This area was settled by French trappers, mountain men, trailblazers and missionaries. Kansas City grew up with the help of risk takers—land speculators, merchants and trail outfitters who catered to a diverse and rough clientele.

From the first white settlement, and long before, there were Native Americans here: Kansas, Osage, Shawnee,

Wyandotte and Delaware. Some had met at the river's junction for centuries to trade, while others had been forced or bribed to move here from lands far to the east. There were Mexicans who brought trade from Santa Fe. African Americans, some free but most of them slaves, were here from the town's beginnings as well. For most of the nineteenth century, one could leave Kansas City and go west for hundreds of miles without hitting a large community, let alone a city. The town was like a port at the edge of a vast prairie sea. The diverse group of inhabitants, along with waves of immigrants constantly coming to or through the city, gave it a unique character.

Today, Kansas City is more than one city. The Greater Kansas City area includes Kansas City, Missouri, the largest city in Missouri; Kansas City, Kansas, the third-largest city in Kansas; Independence, Missouri, the fourth-largest city in Missouri; and dozens of other towns and cities, large and small, from Peculiar up to Roosterville.

Kansas Citians experienced the settlement of the West firsthand, including the fur trade, the steamboat era, the pioneer trails, the fight against slavery, the cattle drives and the railroad connecting East and West. All these shaped the character of the people here. From Old West–style shootouts in the streets to Civil War battles raging through town to political corruption and gangland murder, Kansas City has had more than its share of wild times. All the while, there was the steady push forward of visionary leaders to keep the city on track.

Preface

There have been countless books written to tell the story of Kansas City history, but not every story fits in a standard form. Wrong turns, diversions, embarrassments and odd instances that don't fit in the forward march of civilization don't usually make it into the final draft.

These are the forgotten stories of Kansas City's wild youth—forgotten events and forgotten individuals who marched to a different beat. Tucked away in out-of-print books, boxed up in archives and chronicled in old newspapers (many of which are just now becoming accessible via the Internet), these stories are just itching to be told.

As part of The History Press's Forgotten Tales series, *Forgotten Tales of Kansas City* presents the offbeat, the weird and the lost or forgotten stories of Kansas City's past.

Forgotten Tales of Kansas City

Partly Cloudy with a Chance of Warts?

In the July 12, 1873 issue of *Scientific American*, it was reported that Kansas City had experienced a shower of frogs that "darkened the air and covered the ground for a long distance." Freak storms of fish, snakes and other small critters, like the "frog storm" in Kansas City, have been noted periodically across the globe. They are thought to be caused by waterspouts or tornados lifting animals or objects suddenly and then depositing them some distance away. A few weird downpours have even been reported elsewhere in Missouri. In Independence on June 9, 1907, there was a fish storm, where it was estimated that nearly a ton of small silver-colored fish fell from the sky and covered the town square. Residents picked them up by the handful as souvenirs. On July 4, 1995, a tornado picked up

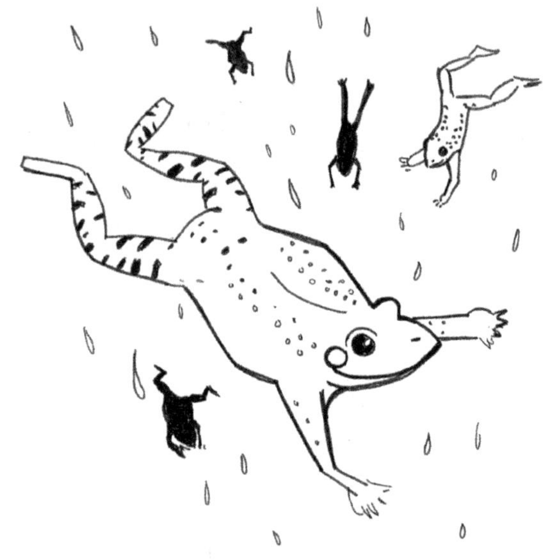

a number of unopened cans of cola from the Double Cola bottling plant in Moberly, Missouri, and deposited them over 150 miles away in Keokuk, Iowa. On November 6, 1943, a storm of over two hundred geese fell on the town of Galena in southern Missouri, possibly as victims of a lightning strike.

Kansas City, by comparison, got off lucky with its amphibious aerial assault, as frog legs are considered a delicacy, while the residents of Galena said the geese that pelted their community had an odd electrical taste, and Independence's fish weren't big enough to be keepers. There were no reports of the explosive results of Iowans opening cans of cola that had been through a tornado—but it would have made a great video.

Night of the Falling Stars

On the night of November 12, 1833, a meteor shower like no other lit up the sky over northwest Missouri. Meteorites fell by the tens of thousands; estimates ran as high as 200,000 per hour. In the little communities along the Missouri River, people watched in awe, and many wondered if the aerial pyrotechnics weren't some sort of sign from heaven. Fear or joy at the approach of apocalypse gripped those men who had professed religion, as well as those who hadn't, a few hours before. The celestial fireworks came about as the result of Earth passing through the tail of a comet, later named Tempel-Tuttle after the astronomers who discovered it. It was an intersection that had happened often before (but never so spectacularly) and is now known as the Leonid meteor shower.

But on that night, the unparalleled display made many wonder if heaven and earth were at odds. The founder of the Mormon religion, Joseph Smith, saw and commented on the event: "I arose, and to my great joy, beheld the stars fall from heaven like a shower of hailstones; a literal fulfillment of the word of God, as recorded in the Holy Scriptures, and a sure sign that the coming of Christ is close at hand." However, in Jackson County, and more specifically, in the county seat at Independence, many locals felt that the fire and brimstone in the sky was more likely a sign that they should rid themselves of these strange new neighbors with their odd beliefs. The singular experience excited superstition and fear in many and was used to justify the expulsion of hundreds of Mormon settlers from Jackson County.

Ghost Town

The largest town in northwest Missouri in 1838 wasn't Kansas City; neither was it Independence or any other town that exists today. The population was more than three thousand, and few of its inhabitants had lived there more than a year. Yet it was a ghost town by 1839.

Platted as a place of refuge and as compensation for losses incurred by Mormons driven from Jackson County, the town of Far West became a beacon for members of the Mormon faith. Building began in 1836, and by 1838, there was a thriving community with several stores and homes. Big plans for expansion were in place, and prophet and church leader Joseph Smith Jr. himself had relocated there from the group's former headquarters in Kirtland, Ohio. At Far West, the church changed its name to the Church of Jesus Christ of Latter-day Saints, and Joseph Smith revealed to members that the Garden of Eden had been in Jackson County but that when Adam and Eve were driven out, they came northeast to Caldwell and Daviess Counties.

As the settlers grew in numbers, some bought land in nearby Carroll and Daviess Counties and once again ran into resistance and conflict with their neighbors. A member of the church had established a ferry across the Grand River, and after visiting the spot in the spring of 1838, Joseph Smith revealed to his followers that in biblical times Adam had built stone altars there after leaving the Garden of Eden. He called the place Adam-on-di-Amon, which he said translated from Egyptian to mean "Adam in the presence of God." (Non-Mormon neighbors shortened the name over time to di-Amon, then Diamond.) Settlement began near the ferry, and the community of Adam-on-di-Amon quickly grew to a population of 1,500. In nearby Gallatin, some residents, fearing a political takeover of the county, tried to prevent their new neighbors from voting in the August election.

The Mormons fought back and won the battle but ultimately would face the state militia in what was called the 1838 Mormon War. Non-Mormon vigilantes began attacking Mormon farms, and when the Mormons formed their own militias to combat the vigilantes, threat and counter-threat turned to attack and counterattack. Finally, the state militia was called out by Governor Lilburn Boggs and charged with removal or extermination of the Mormons. Settlers were forced out of Adam-on-di-Amon. Many took refuge in Far West, swelling its population to nearly that of St. Louis. The town was under siege, and rather than risk a bloodbath, Smith and other Mormon leaders surrendered and were arrested. Smith was indicted, but he was allowed to escape while being transported to be tried in a different venue. By 1839, the Mormon settlements in Missouri had been largely abandoned as the group followed Smith out of the state and moved its headquarters to Nauvoo, Illinois.

Some 170 years later, the ground the once-thriving town occupied is still mostly farmland, but in recent years the Far West Historical Society has opened a country store and has made plans to redevelop the area for historical tourism.

Plague and Prayer

In 1874, they came—a swarm of locusts eating crops and everything else in their path. The invasion of Rocky Mountain locusts (a small-winged grasshopper averaging just a little over one inch long) stopped just short of Missouri, laying their eggs fifty miles west of the border in Kansas.

In the spring of 1875, they hatched. The young locusts crawled through the fields eating everything they could find. Crews had to clear piles of insects from the railroad tracks for the trains to move. The slime of millions of locusts greased the rails and slowed the train's progress. In May, the swarms took wing; billions of insects in a swath one hundred miles wide and another hundred long would fill the sky and were likened to a blizzard, blocking out light.

On the ground, in the fields, the busy jaws made a sound loud enough to hear, similar to a prairie fire, and the damage in their wake was as great if not greater. One farmer reported the locusts eating fifteen acres of corn down to the ground in just three hours. In Independence, the fence around the courthouse kept the creatures out, but it took fifteen wheelbarrow loads piled full, with two hundred pounds of locusts in each, to haul the attackers away.

By late May, cattle were being driven out of the state to save them from starvation. It was reported that the insects were eating the wool off sheep in the fields, stripping trees of leaves and bark and even consuming leather goods and clothing. Governor Charles Henry Hardin had to do something. He had written to Frederick Watts (the U.S. commissioner of agriculture) requesting assistance for the counties that make up the Kansas City area, saying, "Almost every green substance has been consumed." Hardin asked Watt for seeds to help the suffering farmers replant their lost fields. In addition to taking pragmatic steps to help the people of Missouri, Hardin was a man of faith, so he asked his fellow Missourians to turn to prayer. At his request, June 3, 1875, was set aside as a day of prayer and fasting. Skeptics called it his "Grasshopper Proclamation."

However, church congregations across the state responded to the governor's request, and within days of the proclamation, rain came. The insects were knocked down; millions were washed down streams, and the rest were grounded. Then came the wind. Grasshoppers dried their wings and then caught the breeze north and west, leaving Missouri behind. By June 15, 1875, the state was free of the scourge that had destroyed over $100 million in crops. The grasshoppers have returned to Kansas City occasionally, but never again in such numbers.

Pistol-Packing Preacher and His Fierce Flock

Traveling or street preachers occasionally set up shop on a corner in Kansas City today just as they would one hundred years ago. But in December 1908, Kansas City juvenile court officer George Holt spotted a singularly unusual group near the city market singing hymns and collecting money. It included a woman and some school-age children. When the officer asked the woman why the children were evangelizing instead of going to school, she fired back, "What business of yours is it?" The woman

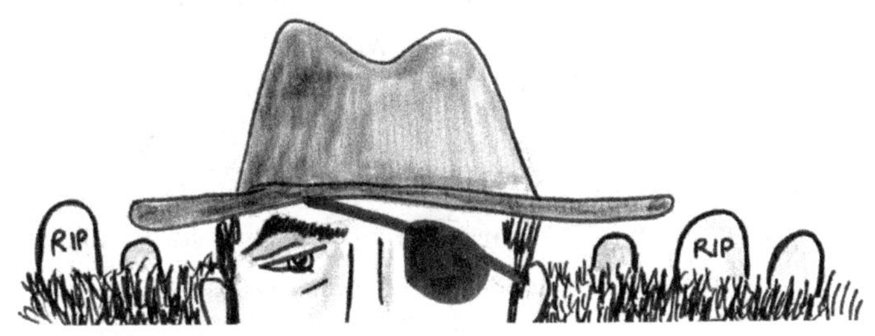

identified herself as Melissa Sharp and explained that she and her husband, James Sharp, along with another couple and their children, were traveling evangelists who lived in a houseboat tied up on the south bank of the Missouri River. She then led the children off, cursing the officer as she went up to the Workingmen's Mission at 309 Main, where James Sharp held religious services.

Officer Holt followed the group to the mission, where he encountered Sharp, who introduced himself as Adam God, the father of Jesus Christ. Sharp cursed and threatened Holt, saying he would kill him and any other police who got in his way. Sharp's partner, Louis Pratt, joined the group, and he and the Sharps all drew pistols on the officer. James Sharp hit the officer in the head with his pistol, and then the children began scratching and hitting Holt as well. Holt, his head bleeding, retreated to the nearby police station. The group of evangelists followed. The children, ranging from ages four to fourteen, were all carrying firearms as well. The evangelists gathered across from the police station. At the southwest corner of Fourth and Main, they began singing hymns, holding on to their pistols all the while. A large crowd of onlookers gathered to see what the commotion was about. By this time, Holt had reported the incident, and another officer, Albert O. Dalbow, was sent to speak to the group. As Dalbow was talking to Sharp, a police lieutenant stepped in behind him, pointed a gun over his shoulder and ordered the evangelists to drop their weapons. Pratt fired, striking Dalbow several times and wounding the lieutenant. Dalbow staggered away and died while several officers came out of the station to help. The streets cleared as police and the evangelicals and their children joined in the fray.

Bullets flew. A saloon window, a horse, a wagon driver's hat and a retired farmer all were hit by the gunfire. The farmer, A.J. Selsor, died. James Sharp slashed one police officer with a knife. Officer Michael Mullane shot Pratt in the leg, only to be chased down and shot himself by Melissa Sharp and one of the Pratt daughters. Pratt was down but not out; he shot police detective Patrick Clark twice from the ground. Another police lieutenant fired at Pratt from a window in police headquarters, taking him out of the fight permanently. Sharp's gun was shot out of his hand, wounding him in the process. With both Pratt and Sharp injured, Melissa Sharp led the children in retreat. Running with gun in hand, she headed north on Delaware but was tackled and captured by three policemen at Third Street. She and twelve-year-old Lena Pratt were arrested, but thirteen-year-old Lulu and eleven-year-old Mary Pratt escaped to the houseboat, where their mother, Della Pratt, was waiting.

Police demanded their surrender, but they refused. Della Pratt and the two girls got off the houseboat onto a skiff, poling out into the icy waters of the Missouri. Police fired at the waterline of the skiff, hoping to sink it. Then they commandeered a ferry to continue the pursuit. When they got to the skiff, Della and Mary Pratt had slipped overboard, trying to avoid the fire from shore. Lulu, who had hidden in the bottom of the boat, had a head wound; she died before they could get her ashore. James Sharp managed to escape but was captured two days later hiding in a haystack on a farm in Johnson County. Weak from running and loss of blood, he surrendered without a fight. James Sharp was convicted of second-degree murder for the death of Officer Mullane. Melissa Sharp was declared insane, and her charges were dismissed.

The shootout left five dead and several wounded (including Officer Clark, who lost an eye in the fight), easily surpassing the damage of more famous gunfights (such as Tombstone's little tussle at the O.K. Corral). James Sharp served fourteen years in prison, returned to preaching from a houseboat and then moved to Joplin, where he continued working as an evangelist until his death in 1946. At his wife's request, he was buried with no services, ritual or minister.

Don't Mess with These Nuns

Independence has had its share of criminals and a long history of tough-on-crime lawmen. It also has had a tradition of compassion and service to its prisoners stretching back to the 1880s, when Mother Mary Jerome Shubrick aided prisoners at the 1859 Jackson County Jail in Independence. Then, as now, the nuns have been involved in helping the wayward of the community. However, walking around with a gun through the bean field at Saint Francis of the Holy Eucharist Convent in Independence is probably not the best way to stay on the good side of the sisters living there.

On August 13, 2009, a pair of nuns spotted a man who appeared to be dragging something through their field and holding a gun in his hand. The two drove over to the man in the convent's Honda Civic. Sister Catarina de Silva wanted to talk to him, thinking he might be a trespassing hunter. When Sister Catarina and Sister Connie Boulch got to the field, they found Corey D. Anderson dragging a rifle, a handsaw and a pair of boxing gloves. After a few minutes of being grilled by the nuns, Anderson dropped everything and ran away.

Sister Catarina, wearing her brown ankle-length habit and a pair of sandals, chased him behind a greenhouse, while Sister Boulch called police on her cellphone. Anderson was already being sought in connection with a pair of burglaries reported earlier that morning.

Once police arrived, the suspect, tired from the pursuit and trying to hide from the nuns, was quickly apprehended. One report even said that the nuns helped police cuff him. Rumors that wooden rulers were used in subduing the suspect have not been substantiated.

Off the Wagon

One hundred years ago, Kansas City firemen had a rough job. Many safety features that are commonplace in homes and businesses today did not exist then. Coal and wood were still used to heat and cook in many homes, and trash was burned outdoors. There was something burning all the time. Smoke inhalation, flames and fire-weakened structures have always been part of the challenge of being a firefighter. But in the beginning of the last century, the ride to work was an exceptionally dangerous undertaking as well.

In 1910, the Kansas City Fire Department had not yet adopted the automobile to get to fires, though it had to share the streets with cars. The trip to a fire was atop a horse-drawn wagon, and the flashing lights and sirens of today were not in use then to clear traffic; rather, a clanging bell was all there was to warn of the wagon's approach. Barreling through crowded streets toward a blazing inferno, hauled by frightened animals with minds of their own, the drivers had to negotiate around fast-moving cars and oil-treated streets on which hooves often slipped.

In December, assistant fire chief M.M. Mahoney of Station 22 in Kansas City was involved in two separate accidents just trying to get to fires. On December 1, 1910, his buggy collided with an automobile, and he was thrown out onto the ground. He was only slightly injured, so he gamely brushed himself off and went on to the fire.

On December 15, he collided with a grocery wagon and was again thrown to the pavement, injuring his shoulder and scraping his face. An ambulance was sent, but by the time it got there, Mahoney had gone on from the accident to the fire.

On December 22, 1909, three firemen were injured while heading toward a fire in a restaurant at the city market. Number 3 hose wagon was drawn by two horses and was making the turn at Tenth Street and Baltimore Avenue when it hit a ditch so hard that it bounced back out and threw the three firemen onboard through the air. Captain M.E. Gaffey's head was cut, Lieutenant George Monahan's right leg was sprained and driver W.L. Grooms's shoulder was sprained. The frightened horses dashed east on Tenth to Main and ran into a trolley pole there, throwing them both to the ground. One horse was uninjured, but the other, named Buffalo, which had served the department for nine years, had a broken leg and had to be put down.

In 1909, a trial run of an automobile hose wagon received the enthusiastic support of the firefighters who witnessed it, especially from the older firemen who had spent years traveling in the dangerous old horse-drawn vehicles. The first vehicles were reserved for the fire chief and assistant fire chief.

It took time and money to make the change, but eventually the hose wagons were replaced by larger, faster, louder, more powerful fire trucks that could carry more hose, more men and more rescue equipment than two or three hose companies. By 1912, the city had several chief's cars with thirty-five-gallon chemical tanks and a couple hose and chemical trucks in use. Besides the advantages in speed and safety, the cars saved the city $1,800 a year in horse-shoeing bills. The Kansas City Fire Department's last horse team made its final emergency run in 1927.

Sailing the High Prairie

The vast grasslands west of Kansas City spread out like an inland sea before the nineteenth-century traveler. One man in particular found the similarity tantalizing. William Thomas came to Kansas City in 1853 with a dream of harnessing the power of the wind to propel settlers across the plains and raise his fortunes as well. Little is known about Thomas. He was believed to be from New England; an experienced sailor, he was

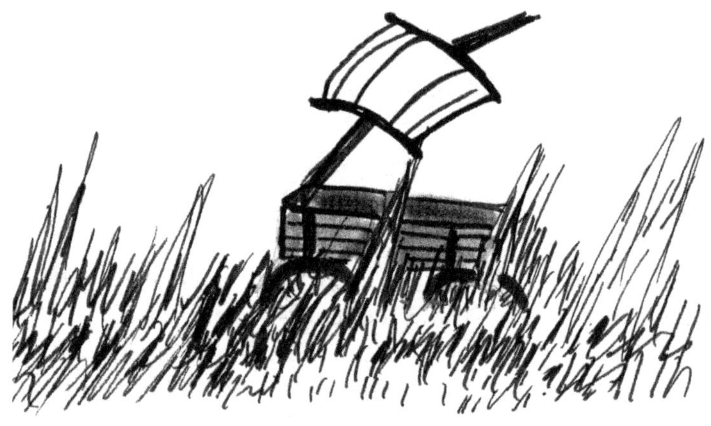

variously called Admiral, Professor or just Windwagon Thomas. He had a dream, and after making a two-hundred-plus-mile round trip from Westport to Council Grove and back in a trial model of his wind wagon, he found men in the town of Kansas who were willing to help him see it through.

Thomas proposed building a larger prototype for a fleet of wind wagons to sail from Westport to Santa Fe. The wind wagons would move faster than animal-drawn wagons; would not require food, water or rest as oxen or mules do; and would not be stranded by the death or theft of an animal. Six Westport businessmen joined Thomas in forming the Westport and Santa Fe Overland

Navigation Company. With the help of Westport wagon shop owner Henry Sager, Thomas designed a twenty-five-foot-long wind wagon with twelve-foot-tall wheels that he had built in a brass foundry in Independence. The wagon, along with the investors and several interested citizens, was pulled out on the plains by oxen. The sail was raised, and the ship began to move. All was going well until Thomas tried to turn the wagon into the wind. A sudden change in the wind sent the wagon hurling across the plains backward. The wagon tumbled on, continuing to pick up speed and lose investors as one by one the men were bounced overboard or voluntarily abandoned ship.

Dr. J.W. Parker, who had come to watch but not ride the wind wagon, tried to follow the speeding calamity, but in a 1905 *Kansas City Star* interview, he said he couldn't keep up: "It was one of the most laughable things I ever saw. But the wagon could go! I had one of the best saddle mules in the country and he could not hold a candle to that wagon." Finally, with only the captain on board, the ship hit a ditch and caught in a fence near Turkey Creek. The ship was destroyed, but Thomas was uninjured. The company of men's dreams of easy riches was dashed, and upon reaching Westport, the disgusted Thomas loaded his original ship and sailed out of town, never to be heard from again.

EXPLODING COWS?

Oscar C. Arnold was one of four children of Wesley Arnold. All four had grown up in the family home on Liberty Street in Independence. Built before the Civil War, the house had once been commandeered as headquarters for Confederate general Jo Shelby during the second Battle of Independence, where it also served as a hospital/morgue. The battle raging through the streets of town was fierce, and it produced a steady business for the surgeons in the home—and for the gravediggers.

By the 1920s, the house was elderly, as was Oscar, the only family member still living there. But Oscar did not live alone. He had a pet cow that was his near and dear companion. Whenever Oscar's cow got sick, he brought it into his home, keeping it in the kitchen and nursing it back to health. However, the last time Oscar's cow got sick, he couldn't save her. She passed away in the kitchen, and a grieving Oscar kept her there for several days.

Finally, mourning was trumped by the need for breathable air. With the help of his friend Raymond Blake, Oscar tried to remove the cow from the kitchen. Unfortunately, the wait had been too long, and she was stiff and bloated. As the two men pushed on the cow, trying to get it through the door, the body burst open, spilling liquids and gases all over the kitchen and the men.

Oscar's friend was gone, but he still had good neighbors, including a group of nuns living in the convent nearby.

When Oscar passed away, he left his home to the sisters, and it was eventually removed to its present location on Main Street. The current owners are aware of their home's grisly past but happily report it to be free of exploding bovines and Confederate raiders for the past several years.

From Slavery to Royalty

The annual American Royal livestock show, horse show and rodeo now hosts half a dozen horse shows, including the UPHA National Championship. Over 250,000 people attend the various events at the Royal each year. Though millions of people from all over the world have attended the show over its more than one hundred years, few know much about the man who came up with the idea in the first place. Tom Bass was born a slave in January 1859. His father, William Hayden Bass, was also his owner. He grew up on one of the largest plantations in Missouri, spending much of his time working and playing in the large stable there. It was there, as a child, that Tom first discovered his exceptional ability to train horses. Strangely enough, he first demonstrated it with a mule. At the age of nine, Tom had been given charge of a particularly stubborn mule that seemed determined not to behave for anyone on the plantation. Tom surprised everyone when he not only trained the mule to take a rider but also to cantor and walk backward for him.

After the Civil War, Tom stayed on at the plantation but found work in town driving a wagon to take guests from the train station to the hotel. Tom's reputation for dealing with problem horses began to spread, as locals started bringing their ornery and difficult animals to him and getting them back trained and ready to work. Tom also had a good eye for picking quality horses, and he began work at age twenty for Joseph Potts at the Mexico Horse Sales Company, helping select horses to buy and then training them. While working for Potts, Tom invented a bit that was more humane than those being used at the time. It became widely popular, though Tom made no attempt to patent or take a profit from it. His concern for the well-being of the animals in his charge, and patience and kindness in training them, was what set him apart from many trainers of his day.

In 1883, Tom went into business for himself, buying a few acres and training and selling horses. His reputation grew, and he could count the governor of Missouri among his clients by 1888. Tom's reputation soared a few years later, when he entered a gelding he had trained in the St. Louis Horse Show. Tom was the first black man ever to compete in the show. He and his horse, Columbus, so astounded the judges and contestants with their performance that they won first place, in spite of prejudice against them. Later that year, Buffalo Bill Cody came to Tom's home and convinced Tom to let him buy Columbus for his *Wild West Show*. Cody would not be the only famous person to make the pilgrimage to Tom's farm. Will Rogers, Teddy Roosevelt and a host of others also sought his help. Tom became so well known that he was invited to and rode in three presidential inaugurations and met five U.S. presidents. Tom's talent gave him unprecedented opportunities, even at a time when Jim Crow laws were enforced and racism barred him from some competitions.

In 1893, Tom moved his operation to Kansas City. In 1894, he was given the opportunity to sit on the advisory board for the Kansas City Fire Department. The board wanted to raise money to send fire chief George C. Hale to Europe to study different breeds of fire horses and participate in an international fireman competition. Tom suggested that the fire department sponsor a horse show to help fund the chief's trip. The board, knowing Tom's participation would help draw crowds and raise money, voted in favor of his proposal. The result was the first Kansas City Horse Show, and many of the participants were inspired by Tom's idea to bring a world-class competition to the Kansas City area.

Eventually, they formed the American Royal Cattle Show (started in 1899) and added a horse show in 1907. Tom was the only black man allowed to participate in the Royal in those early days. He lived to see and take part in many American Royal competitions. The addition of the

American Royal parade and the formation of the Future Farmers of America during the 1928 Royal helped fix the event permanently on Kansas City's calendar before Tom's death in 1934.

Big Name

The nineteenth-century showman P.T. Barnum is credited with saying, "There's a sucker born every minute" and "You can fool some of the people all of the time, and all of the people some of the time, but you can't fool all the people all of the time." Barnum had a way with words, especially to promote his shows. In 1882, he had a new attraction that would add a word to the vocabulary of Americans from coast to coast: a giant African bush elephant named Jumbo that Barnum had purchased from the London Zoo. Standing ten feet, nine inches at the shoulder and eating two hundred pounds of hay, two bushels of oats, a barrel of potatoes, ten loaves of bread and two or more quarts of onions a day, as well as drinking an occasional keg of beer, Jumbo was a sensation. He was a major fan attraction everywhere he went, and as part of Barnum's show, he was seen all over the United States and Canada.

But Jumbo only came to Kansas City one time. In 1882, Barnum's show stayed mostly in the eastern states, and in

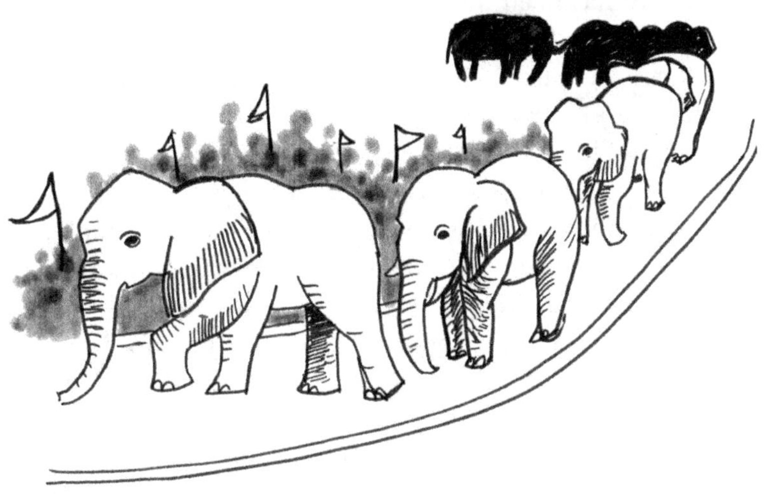

1883, it only made it as close as Hannibal, Missouri. But for one day only, October 3, 1884, Jumbo led a parade of forty elephants through the streets of Kansas City. "The menagerie was a wonderland, with its army of elephants, with the gigantic 'Jumbo' and the sacred white elephant leading in point of interest," gushed the *Kansas City Journal*. The parade came down Main to Nineteenth, then over and back up Grand and then back down Main to the fairgrounds. There were two shows that day, and over twelve thousand people filled the tent at the afternoon performance. According to the next day's *Journal*, "Altogether the show was a grand success."

There has been much debate as to the origin of the word "jumbo"; there is a similar Congolese word that means elephant, two Swahili words (*jumbe* meaning "chief" and *jambo* meaning "hello"), a Zulu word (*jumba* meaning "large package") and the Mandingo word for a "masked dancer" (*maamajomboo*). Though any of these African sources are possible, in America the word jumbo appeared rarely in print before Barnum's promotion of the pachyderm, after which it became synonymous with anything extraordinarily large. The Barnum and Bailey circus traveled thousands of miles each year, and trains were the means to that end. In April 1885, Jumbo was hit and killed by a train, purportedly while trying to steer a younger elephant off the tracks (Barnum's version of the event). Not one to miss an opportunity, Barnum had the giant stuffed and displayed with the circus for two more years.

Later, Jumbo's bones were donated to the Museum of Natural History, and his stuffed carcass was put in the Barnum Museum at Tufts College in Medford, Massachusetts, where he became the school's mascot. Students would toss coins in his trunk, pat him or tug his tail for good luck before games or tests.

In 1975, fire reduced Jumbo's remains to ashes, except for his tail. Some of Jumbo's ashes were collected, and fourteen ounces were placed in a Peter Pan crunchy peanut butter jar that is still kept on the desk of the school's athletic director. Jumbo's tail remains in the school's museum.

Though he spent only a day in Kansas City, he gained a permanent place in the vocabulary here. In fact, his name is seen by Kansas City baseball fans at every Royals game. One of the largest stadium screens in professional sports is the 84-foot-wide by 105-foot-high "jumbotron" at Royals stadium. Fans keep track of the score and watch replays on it while eating jumbo-sized bags of cotton candy or jumbo hot dogs or drinking jumbo-sized beverages.

He Never Missed an Appointment

David Rice Atchison was admitted to the Kentucky bar in 1829 and then opened a law office near Kansas City at Liberty, Missouri, in 1830. His practice flourished there. His best-known client was Mormon leader Joseph Smith, whom he represented in several land disputes. Atchison soon became involved in politics, running successfully for the Missouri House of Representatives in 1834. He served in a number of public offices in subsequent years, being appointed to one office after another. Atchison was appointed major general in the state militia in 1838 during Missouri's Mormon War. Three years later, he was appointed circuit court judge for the six counties of the Platte Purchase. He then was appointed as county commissioner in Platte County.

In October 1843, the thirty-six-year-old Atchison was appointed to the United States Senate to fill a vacancy left by the death of Lewis F. Lynn, subsequently finishing Lynn's term of office. At age thirty-eight he was chosen as president pro tempore of the Senate. While serving in that capacity, it has been argued that he might have been president for a day. On March 4, 1849, outgoing president James K. Polk's term was expired, and the incoming president, Zachary Taylor, refused to take the oath of office on the fourth because it was a Sunday. Polk's vice-presidential pick, Millard Fillmore, also had not been sworn in. Atchison, the serving president pro tempore of the Senate, was next in line of succession. Atchison himself doubted that he had any legal claim to the presidency. Taylor was sworn in the next day, so Atchison's questionable term was only for a day.

Atchison's appointments didn't end with the ascension of President Taylor. On April 18, 1853, while serving again as president pro tempore, Atchison was appointed vice president of the United States, replacing William R. King, who had died in office. He served as vice president to Franklin Pierce until December 4, 1854. In the 1850s, Atchison had been a leader of the Missouri "border ruffians," who had invaded Kansas to elect a pro-slavery legislature, using any means necessary. Atchison's pro-slavery sentiments led him to accept an appointment as a general in the Missouri State Guard during Missouri's secession dispute. After the Battle of Pea Ridge, Atchison resigned his commission and retired to his farm near Plattsburg, Missouri. David Rice Atchison served as judge, general, U.S. senator, vice president of the United States for over a year and perhaps even as president without any of the expense or tedium of campaigning or running for office. He just showed up for all his appointments.

Out of Sight

The limestone deposits underneath Kansas City have been a source for building materials since settlers first came to the area. Large deposits were mined at first for building stones and later for gravel for roads and concrete mix (especially for the Pendergast Ready Mix Company). There are more than half a dozen larger underground complexes. The largest, Hunt Midwest's Subtropolis, is a 1940s mining operation that was retasked in the 1960s. This massive facility is the largest underground business park in the world, taking up nearly twice the area of Rome's catacombs.

One hundred feet below ground, ten thousand limestone pillars secure the ceiling over six miles of road, two miles of rail lines and five million square feet of office and warehouse space. With twenty-five million square feet of underground facilities, Kansas City utilizes more ground below the surface than upstairs in the downtown business district. The ideal weather conditions—dry but overcast with temperatures in the sixties—have enticed a number of businesses and government agencies to store important items they want to protect there. The United States Postal Service uses one facility to store hundreds of millions of commemorative stamps. The Kansas City Missouri Department of Parks, Recreation and Boulevards stores blueprints, documents and a collection of odd-looking old building ornaments in another. Grantham University and Jaeger's Paintball facility are both underground as well.

In February 2008, one of the most unusual items to be stored under Kansas City arrived in a truck from Fort Worth, Texas, that was driven personally by NARA administrator Reed Whitaker: the contents of Parkland Trauma room No. 1, the room where President John F. Kennedy died. Purchased and dismantled by the federal government thirty-five years earlier, all the room's contents, even the door and floor tiles, were put into storage in a locked vault in a Fort Worth, Texas warehouse administered by the NARA.

Now, the contents are tucked somewhere in NARA's Kansas City facility known as the "caves." Whitaker said of the room, "Basically, it's not to be examined, not to be shown to the press, not to be photographed, not to be exhibited to the public" and "it's in a secure location." That's the kind of reassuring remark that keeps conspiracy theorists blogging till the wee hours. What else might be stored in the caves? Maybe aliens from Roswell? Or the studio where the moon landings were faked?

Jesse James and John F. Kennedy Rob a Train—Together?

In 1899, John F. Kennedy and Jesse James were facing trial in Kansas City for allegedly robbing Missouri Pacific Train No. 5 just outside Kansas City in Leeds, Missouri. John Fitzgerald "Jack" Kennedy (born over forty years before the U.S. president who shared his name) was a Kansas City–area tough from the Cracker Neck district south of Independence, Missouri. His alleged partner in crime, Jesse James Jr., was the son of the notorious outlaw who had been killed seventeen years earlier by a member of his own gang.

Jesse Jr. ran a cigar store in the Jackson County Courthouse in downtown Kansas City and counted former governor Thomas Crittenden and future president Harry Truman among his regular customers. The train robbery was a botched job in which six men had boarded the train, detached the engine, drove it a mile away and blew up the safe—a little too well, destroying most of its contents.

Kennedy had experience as a locomotive engineer, James had the notorious name and both had been implicated by an accused gang member who had cracked under interrogation. Jesse James Jr. was to be tried first; the prosecutor, James A. Reed, was undefeated and was confident that he had sufficient evidence to prove his case. Politics and public sympathy intervened. An election was

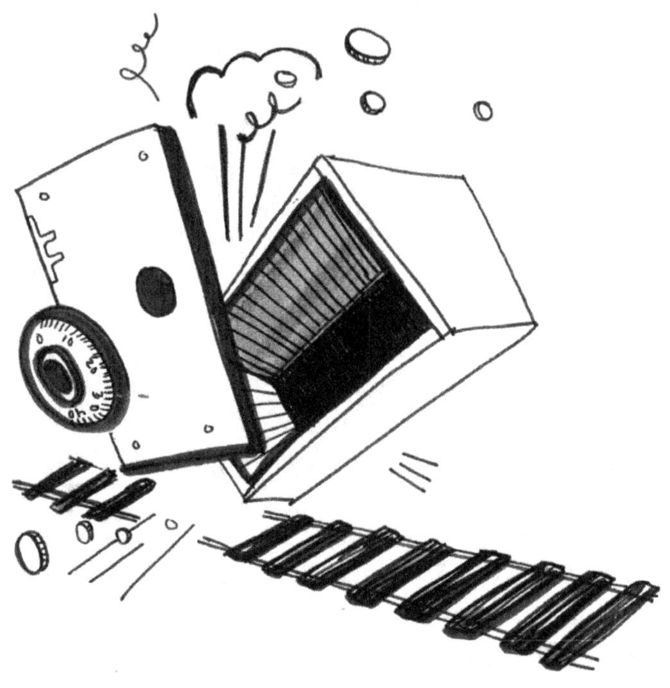

only weeks away. A number of prominent Democrats saw the case as an opportunity to play on public sympathy and came out in support of Jesse. Republican attacks backfired when they called the Democrats guerrillas and train robbers; some Democrats embraced the moniker and started opening their speeches with the line: "Fellow train robbers."

The judge selected for the case, fearing his own reelection chances, avoided service of the notice to appear, and thus the trial was postponed until after the election—which the Democrats won. James was offered the services and advice of the city's best defense lawyers, especially those with political ambitions. He selected Frank Walsh, who successfully swayed the jury, parading prominent citizens and the extended James family through the witness stand. Jesse Jr.'s grandmother, who lost an arm and a son to "unfair persecution"; mother, who lost a husband to state-sponsored murder; and Uncle Frank, who had been acquitted in his own trials and then lived within the law ever since, were all in attendance.

Sympathy was garnered for the family and the defendant by Attorney Walsh, who painted the prosecution as a persecution of a member of a family already wronged by the state. The jury deliberated less than an hour, and acquitted James. Reed, perhaps sensing the political mood of the day, dropped charges against Kennedy as well. Encouraged by his supporters, Jesse Jr. would eventually go to the Kansas City School of Law, graduating as valedictorian of the class of 1906 and attaining the highest score of all the candidates for the Missouri state bar exam that year. He practiced law in Kansas City, wrote a biography of his father, played his father in two movies, settled in Los Angeles, California, and opened a law office there. His grandson, James Ross, also became a lawyer and eventually a superior court judge in California.

As for John F. Kennedy, he was arrested and convicted only a few months later for another train robbery and sentenced to seventeen years in prison. He was eventually paroled but then was shot in the act of robbing another train south of St. Louis in 1922.

The Cole Younger and Frank James Wild West Show

Frank James is buried in Independence and Cole Younger in Lee's Summit. This area was their stomping grounds, and they had many friends and acquaintances in the communities in and around Kansas City.

Younger had served twenty-five years in prison in Minnesota but was out on a conditional pardon. Frank James had never been convicted of any of the many robberies attributed to the James-Younger gang. This was in part due to the loyalty and silence of those who knew him, including Cole Younger, who had been offered parole if he would name Frank or his brother Jesse as accomplices in the Northfield robbery.

Younger refused to betray his old friend, even at the price of his own freedom. Frank had worked at a variety of jobs after his brother Jesse's death, including shoe salesman and bouncer, and had even tried his hand at acting. Cole was somewhat hamstringed by the conditions of his pardon. He had agreed never to return to the state of Minnesota and not to place himself on public exhibition.

Though they were known to be fellow guerrilla fighters and believed to have been members of the same outlaw gang, the only business that Frank and Cole would admit to working together was their *Wild West Show*. Formerly the *Buckskin Bill Wild West Show*, in 1903, James and Younger gave their names to the program, and Cole purchased a partial interest in it. Frank was hired as arena manager. The men partnered with the former general manager and retained various acts as well, using thirty train cars of equipment from the old show.

Younger purchased one hundred horses from a Kansas City dealer and hired some Kansas City stockyard cowboys to work in the show as broncobusters. *The Cole Younger and Frank James Wild West Show* set out in the spring of 1903, starting the season in Chicago. On the inauspicious opening night, one of Cole Younger's horses was stolen. A man from the crowd jumped on the horse and just brazenly rode it out of the arena. Cowboys from the show chased him, but he managed to escape. The two former guerrillas knew that lending their names to the enterprise would help to drive ticket sales, but in order to keep Cole out of trouble with Minnesota authorities, he officially would only work as bookkeeper and manager.

Frank, however, participated in the performances, firing his guns from the saddle once again. Though Younger was not allowed to perform in the show, he found other ways to use his name and presence to profit. Cole began working as ticket taker, giving attendees a chance to meet him. At the same time, copies of his autobiography were made available to purchase before entering the tent. Of course, having the author handy to sign a copy of the book and meet in person didn't hurt book or ticket sales. The men at least tried to conform to the letter of the law, if not the spirit.

The show came to Kansas City on May 8, 1903. The troupe set up at Fifteenth and Kansas and later gave a street parade, including several cowboys and Indians, three bands and Frank and Cole riding in a carriage. They stayed two days, with Frank rescuing the stagecoach from Indians and showing off his skills with a pistol. The two men continued to tour with the show through the summer, but Frank James, in his sixth decade, tired of the job. The two-shows-a-day schedule followed by sleeping in a moving train at night was wearing him down. Cole and Frank asked to be released from the show in September but were rebuffed by the show's manager. The negotiations purportedly broke down when Cole stuck a gun in the man's face.

The two brought suit against the manager, whom they claimed was allowing grafters and other bad elements into the troupe and had not provided all the equipment he had agreed to. The manager accused Cole of embezzlement and had him arrested in Nevada, Missouri. The cases were ultimately thrown out, and the two sides went their separate ways. Frank took his profits from the show and bought a farm down in Oklahoma, while Cole ended up eventually finding success on the lecture circuit, despite the conditions of his pardon. Cole used his lecture proceeds to buy a home in Lee's Summit, where he retired.

Outlaw Movie Star?

Frank James and Cole Younger weren't the only men from this area who advanced from banditry to show business. A cousin of Cole Younger, Emmett Dalton was born in 1871 near Belton, Missouri (now a growing Kansas City suburb). His father had owned land before the Civil War, but the family had been forced off it, and he was working in Westport as a bartender. The Daltons' fortunes had shrunk as the family grew (fifteen children in all), and they eventually moved to the Coffeeville, Kansas area.

The eldest Dalton, Frank, became a U.S. deputy marshal. Brothers Grat and Bob also became deputy marshals, and younger brother Emmett assisted his brothers on several posses. The death of Frank Dalton in a shootout, and a dispute over payment for their service as lawmen (not to mention easier pickings on the other side of the law), led Bob, Grat and Emmett to form an outlaw gang.

The Daltons' mother was Adeline Younger-Dalton, and the men knew all about their outlaw cousins. Bob Dalton, in particular, felt their gang should try to outshine their famous cousin's notorious accomplishments. Accused of committing a number of robberies, the gang met its downfall in Coffeeville, Kansas, in 1892 in a failed attempt to rob two banks at the same time. The shootout with townspeople left eight men dead, including all the gang members except Emmett, who had twenty-three bullet wounds yet somehow survived. Emmett served fourteen years in prison at Lansing and then was paroled.

By 1910, he was touring with a film about the raid on Coffeeville that he had put together with John B. Tackett, the photographer who had taken pictures of the aftermath of the raid. Many towns banned the program, but it was shown in February 1910 at the Olympic Theater at 1123 Grand Avenue in Kansas City. By 1912, Dalton had moved to Hollywood and made another version of the film, calling it *The Last Stand of the Dalton Boys*.

Dalton continued to tour and lecture against the outlaw life while exhibiting films that showed exciting stories about it. He produced: *When a Man's a Pal*, *Across the Chasm* and *The Man of the Desert* and yet another remake of his story, *Beyond the Law*, which he toured with from 1918 until 1925. In 1919, the *Kansas City Star* reported Emmett had stopped shooting people and had taken to shooting pictures. The paper described Dalton as a movie magnate. In October 1922, Emmett stopped in Kansas City, pausing his trip to New York from Los Angeles to see the Priests of Pallas Parade. He was president of the Standard Pictures Corporation at that time, and the *Star* reporter commented that Dalton had the clothes and bearing of a successful businessman.

By the 1930s, Emmett Dalton was wealthy. Though much of his fortune had come from selling real estate, it was the motion picture business that placed him in Hollywood, where he would find his success. Emmett was one of the first and most successful ex-outlaws to hit Tinsel Town, though he would not be the last.

Other survivors of the Wild West who made a run at movie stardom included Henry Starr, Wyatt Earp, Al Jennings, Buffalo Bill Cody, Jesse James Jr. and Arkansas Tom Jones (aka Roy Daugherty).

REST IN PIECES

I don't know if it's just a Missouri thing, but there sure are a lot of strange stories from below the surface. Blue Eye Missouri has Kenneth Webb's arm buried in its cemetery. Milan, Missouri, has Pete Kibble's foot. Both of those limbs were severed in accidents and then buried, their owners never managing to rejoin them, even in death. Kansas City also has had more than a few odd burials and mass graves, one of which likely includes a stack of over one hundred amputated arms and legs.

In October 1864, the largest Civil War battle west of the Mississippi took place just south of Kansas City along

Brush Creek. The nearby home of John Wornall was used by both Union and Confederate forces as a hospital during the Battle of Westport. There were nearly eight hundred casualties on Wornall Road alone. John Wornall's nine-year-old son, Frank, witnessed the aftermath. He recalled amputations hurriedly done in the house; the severed limbs thrown out the window were piled up to the second story.

In the days that followed, the dead were gathered, and many were unidentifiable. The battle had involved cavalry charges and cannon loaded with canister (giant shotgun-like shells) leaving bullet-riddled, trampled corpses in its wake. Many of the dead lacked uniforms, and some Confederates wore Federal uniforms they had acquired during the war. The casualties outnumbered the population of most of the nearby towns. A mass grave for the unidentified Confederates was dug around Fifty-fifth and Ward Parkway. The amputated limbs likely were hauled in wagons along with the bodies to that site or buried somewhere in the yard of the Wornall home. Other mass graves can be found along the Confederate line of march, near the Little Blue River in the yard of the Lawson-Moore home. Sixteen enlisted men were buried together, and four officers were placed in a separate grave.

Surgeon in chief Ferdinand V. Dayton of the Federal army that had pursued the Confederate raiders through the Kansas City area reported that "it was with great difficulty that the wounded could be collected or the dead buried; in fact at no time, to my knowledge, was a proper burying party detailed, so that I was obliged to use stragglers and hospital attendants to that purpose, and with the aid of citizens I hope that most, if not all, of our killed were interred." The battle raged over thousands of acres of forests, farms, towns and prairie, with little likelihood that a correct casualty count was or even could have been made.

Civil War battles weren't the only source of mass graves in Kansas City. A cholera epidemic in the 1830s and another in the 1850s swept through the area. East of Kansas City, on the plantation of Jabez Smith, several slaves succumbed to the disease and were buried en masse on his property. Also, during the 1918 Spanish flu epidemic, the Jackson County poor farm was inundated with corpses of impoverished Kansas Citians who could not afford burial elsewhere. Graves were dug, and then re-dug, as space ran out. Finally, the dead were buried three to a grave, stacked intermittently, with the top position being only inches below ground. These eerie grave sites coupled with Kansas City's many reputed haunted houses (including the Wornall home) are enough to make even the mildly superstitious tread carefully through town.

Just Shut Up and Play Ball!

Baseball in the 1860s was a relatively new but popular diversion. The rules of the modern game had not been established at that time, and the terminology was a bit different. Back then, Kansas City had a team called the Antelopes that played in a field near Fourteenth and McGee Streets. The ball they used was smaller and harder than modern baseballs, and they didn't wear gloves. The pitcher was called a hurler, and the ball was tossed underhand. The batter was called a striker, and if he hit an "ace" (home run), a cowbell would be rung. If the opposing fielder caught the ball, even after one bounce, the striker was out. If the fielder made an error, it was called a muff. Fans were extremely loyal and often came armed in those days. Rivalries were intense, and drinking, fighting and general mischief were all part of the fun. Umpires who incurred the wrath of the crowd might be pelted with dirt clods or potatoes if they were lucky; more than one had to literally run for his life.

One of Kansas City's rivals for commerce and railroad lines and in baseball was Atchison, Kansas. The team there was known as the Pomeroys, named for former mayor of Atchison and president of the Atchison, Topeka and Santa Fe Railroad: Samuel C. Pomeroy. In 1866, the two teams had met twice before, once in each of their respective towns. Accusations of favoritism were hurled at the umpire of each previous game. The umpire of the game played at Kansas City had to run for his life from the opposing fans. Someone who could not be easily intimidated or swayed needed to be found to judge the next contest.

Enter U.S. deputy marshal "Wild Bill" Hickock. Bill enjoyed going to the Saturday afternoon Antelope games and had a reputation of being tough but fair. Both sides agreed and requested his assistance. Hickock, when asked if he could judge the contest fairly, said, "I'm a U.S. deputy marshal, not one of the local men. I got friends in Atchison, like I got friends here. You got no call to wonder." Hickock studied a borrowed rulebook the day before the game and was familiar with his duties. He was almost late for the contest because he was busy at another game, gambling at Jake Forcade's place. Hickock managed to break away, and on August 12, 1866, he stepped behind the plate and served as umpire. The Antelopes won the contest 48–28. Neither fans nor players from either side chose to dispute any of the deadly umpire's calls; none of the usual catcalls or pelting of the umpire occurred, and it was reported that the game came off without a ripple of disorder.

In fact, it was said that the crowd was as quiet as if they were at a prayer meeting—perhaps they were influenced by the demeanor of the new umpire or at least by his attire. Wild Bill Hickock was armed with a pair of six-shooters, which he wore openly throughout the game. Both sides seemed quite satisfied with the final result, and Hickock was asked what reward he would take for his services. He replied, "Send down to Frank Short's livery for an open hack to take me back to Jake's." He was shortly thereafter carried from the field in an open carriage drawn by two white horses to celebrate at the Market Square, where he could resume drinking and gambling, joyfully followed by a throng of Antelope fans.

How to Rob a Train without Really Trying

In the 1870s, Kansas City was still the western edge of the settled states. Beyond it were small and scattered communities, with long stretches of prairie, desert or mountains between them. Going back east from Kansas City, it was over two hundred miles to St. Louis, and again, towns along the way were small and fairly spread out. One of the little towns about thirty miles east of Kansas City was Odessa, now a growing suburb. A steep incline near town along the railway led to a bright idea by some local outlaws. Members of the gang would buy tickets and board a train coming east from Kansas City.

A special tool in hand, fashioned by a local blacksmith, was used to gain access to one of the train's freight cars. As the train slowed on its uphill climb, members of the gang pushed the contents of the car off the train. Their accomplices, waiting in the woods with wagons, would pick up the free supplies to use, give away or sell for a profit. The outlaws on the train would then reseal the freight car, go back to their seats and calmly get off at a later stop.

This trick worked several times; the railroad had no idea where or when the freight had been removed, so it didn't know where to look for the robbers. Finally, detectives caught up with the gang, but not before it made off with tens of thousands of dollars' worth of loot. The gang had

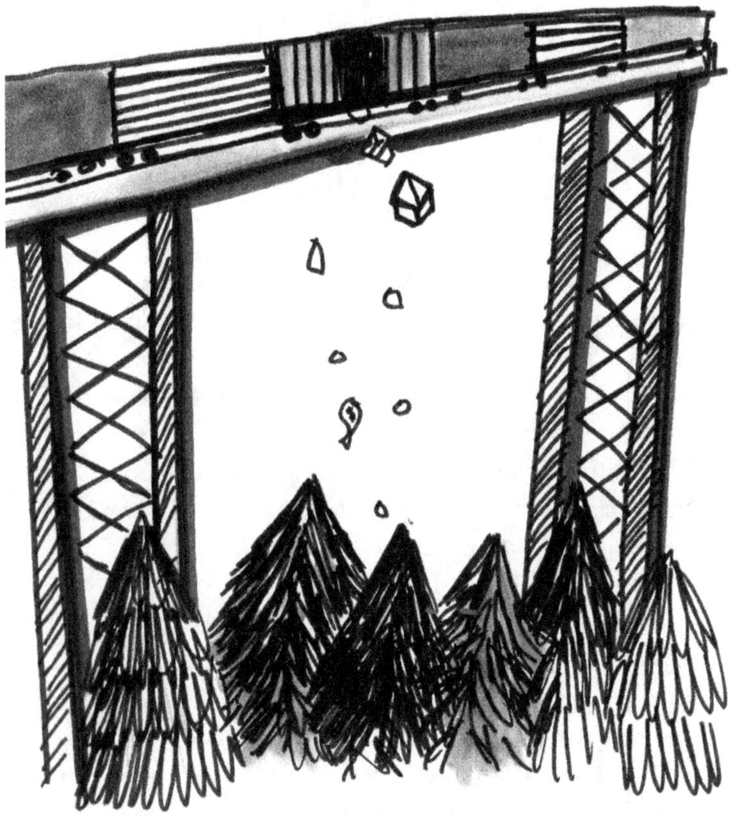

pulled off all its robberies without pulling a gun or harming a single railroad employee.

While researching this story, I found out that my wife is a cousin to several members of this gang (the Reeds) through her maternal great-grandmother.

Know Your Neighbors

Jesse James Jr. wrote a biography of his famous outlaw father, published in 1899, in which he describes several locations in Kansas City where Jesse and his family lived while he was avoiding the long arm of the law. Among these were East Ninth Street between Michigan and Euclid; Troost Avenue between Tenth and Eleventh Streets; and, finally, Woodland Avenue between Twelfth and Thirteenth Streets.

Behind the house on Woodland there was an empty lot, and on the other side of the lot was the home of then Jackson County marshal Con Murphy's father. At that time, Jesse had grown a beard and would walk with a limp, using a cane sometimes. He would wear a long overcoat or in some way or another disguise his looks and sometimes make himself look older than he was.

Each night, Marshal Murphy would gather a posse at his father's home to head out to the country east of town and look for members of the James gang. Jesse Jr. reported, "My father used to walk over to Murphy's house in the evening when the posse would be starting out, and talk to them about their plans and wish them good luck on their trip. I told Mr. Murphy recently about this, and he laughed heartily at it."

Jesse had used disguises often before, and Con Murphy knew he wasn't the first to be fooled by the brazen outlaw. The James boys were wanted from 1866 until 1882 and in all that time avoided being captured by lawmen—even when they were next-door neighbors.

SUING JESSE JAMES

Jesse James started his outlaw career shortly after the Civil War, while he was still a teenager. His tutelage under men like Bloody Bill Anderson and Archie Clement during the war had prepared him for the success he would achieve in his dangerous new occupation. Much of his career took place in and around Kansas City, and many of the outlying communities would receive visits from the outlaw's gang.

In 1869, Jesse was still learning his trade, though, and beginners occasionally make mistakes. When Jesse and his brother Frank rode into the little town of Gallatin, Missouri, his intentions may have been to leave town with a nice haul of stolen money. He may have just planned to kill Samuel Cox, as Cox had led the Union forces that killed Jesse's mentor, Bloody Bill Anderson.

The problem was that Jesse walked into the wrong bank to accomplish either goal; the brothers entered the Daviess County Savings Association. Jesse shot John Sheets, whom he mistook for Cox (who worked at another bank on the square), and in their excitement, the bandits left the building with less than $100. As they left, Jesse proclaimed, "I shot the man who killed Bill Anderson," and they jumped on their horses to ride out of town. But Jesse's horse got spooked and threw him, dragging him with his foot in the stirrup until he untangled himself. A horseless (and probably embarrassed) Jesse had to ride double with his older brother to make his escape. Just outside town, the two came upon farmer Daniel Smoote and relieved him of his horse at gunpoint. Jesse got on the fresh mount, and the brothers rode away, making good their escape. However, Smoote was not one to take things lying down; he wanted his horse, or at least its value, returned. Though few doubted that the bank robber, murderer and horse thief was Jesse James, Smoote had difficulty finding an attorney who would risk his life to file suit against the dangerous outlaw. Finally, a young lawyer named Henry McDougal took Smoote's case.

The James brothers were cautious enough to know that showing up in person in court wasn't a good plan. They hired Samuel Richardson, one of the state's most successful lawyers at the time, to defend them in absentia. Richardson got the first suit dismissed on a technicality, claiming that the Clay County sheriff had failed to deliver notice personally to either of the brothers, only leaving papers at their mother's farm. The story might have ended there, but Jesse had acquired a habit of writing to newspapers. He had a champion in the unreconstructed Confederate editor of the *Kansas City Times*, John Newman Edwards. Edwards had not only defended Jesse to the public but also built him up as a modern-day Robin Hood.

A letter to the newspaper would be published and even have an accompanying editorial praising and defending the outlaw's actions. Perhaps expecting similar treatment in the Gallatin paper, Jesse wrote a letter to the editor in response to its description of the robbery, claiming innocence and that the horse found at the scene was no longer his but had been sold to a "jayhawker." The letter was published, and it gave McDougal an idea. McDougal had a letter of his own published, stating basically that since Jesse clearly read the Gallatin paper, he would no doubt see the public notice of suit and was thus duly served and should attend court. McDougal took this before a judge and found himself settling the case with Frank and Jesse's lawyer. Smoote received the horse Jesse left behind as compensation for his loss. As the outlaw's horse was a Thoroughbred valued at $500 (which could buy eighty acres of land near Gallatin at that time), Smoote definitely got the best of the James boys. McDougal's success brought more business through his law office, and he was twice elected mayor of Gallatin and then served as a probate judge. He eventually became a partner in one of Kansas City's largest law firms.

Marshal Tom

In 1902, a new Jackson County marshal was elected. The man who would later be known as "Boss Tom" and whose machine would run Kansas City and influence state and even national politics was the chief official responsible for law and order in Jackson County. The future boss had the right kind of experience for the job and plenty of backing from his older brother Jim's political machine.

First, he had worked a few years in Jim's saloon doing double duty as bookkeeper and bouncer. Then, with his brother's backing, he was appointed constable of the Kansas City Court in 1894 and then deputy marshal for Jackson County in 1900.

While working as deputy under Marshal Sam Chiles, Tom learned the responsibilities, as well as the benefits, of the marshal's job. Though political influence had gained him the position, he had serious responsibilities, including standing guard overnight for a prisoner (Jim Reed) who was to be hanged the next day.

Tom Pendergast served out his term as deputy for Marshal Chiles and then was elected superintendant of streets. While serving in that position, he beat up a police officer for roughing up a young man from the neighborhood. Tom was a scrapper, and he was not afraid to back his views or his friends with his fists. The office of marshal was an elective position. Tom's brother James had a strong political machine in the city, and it once again helped propel Tom to victory in the race for that job. After presenting his slate of fifteen deputies for approval, and putting up a $10,000 bond, he took the oath of office.

On January 1, 1903, Marshal Tom inspected the jail and was presented with his badge of office; his deputies gave him a diamond-studded gold star. Once in place, Tom was considered a good marshal who treated prisoners humanely. It was reported that Marshal Tom personally bought turkey dinners for all the inmates on Christmas during the two years he was in office. No use making enemies of men who might have a chance to vote for him when they regained their freedom. (Tom continued the tradition later as councilman, his "boys" giving out as many as three thousand free dinners during the holidays.)

Tom Pendergast seemed to enjoy his time in the marshal's position. The first year, he took a ten-day fishing vacation to Colorado. The second year, he went fishing again, without telling his deputies where he was going. While Tom was gone fishing, a man was arrested in Springfield, Missouri, for impersonating the marshal. The man had Tom's Frisco rail pass in his possession and registered at the Metropolitan Hotel as T.J. Pendergast, but under interrogation, he admitted to authorities that he was not the marshal. According to the deputies, Marshal Pendergast's coat had been stolen from the jail a few months earlier, and his Frisco pass was in the pocket.

Political winds changed direction the next election, blowing Tom out of office, but not for long. He would eventually take over his brother's city council position and consolidate power within the Democratic Party in Kansas City, Jackson County and beyond.

A 1907 *Kansas City Star* article stated the general consensus on Tom Pendergast at that time: "He was a success when he held the office of county Marshal and his executive ability is unquestioned." Though Tom is best remembered as the boss of a corrupt political organization with criminal ties, he started out dispensing justice and taking care of his friends and supporters. His rise was gradual, and he knew men from the bottom up. His fall was fast, but when he died, his mourners included people from the top all the way down.

Let Me Out of Here!

Harry Houdini first came to Kansas City by mistake. At age twelve, he had tried to run away from home to find his fortune. He carried with him a shoeshine kit that had helped him contribute to the support of his family since he was eight. He thought he had boarded a train bound for Texas but ended up in Kansas City instead. Somehow, he managed to rejoin his family, as they had moved to New York while he was away.

Houdini returned to Kansas City years later to begin his career on the Orpheum circuit. Finally, in 1900,

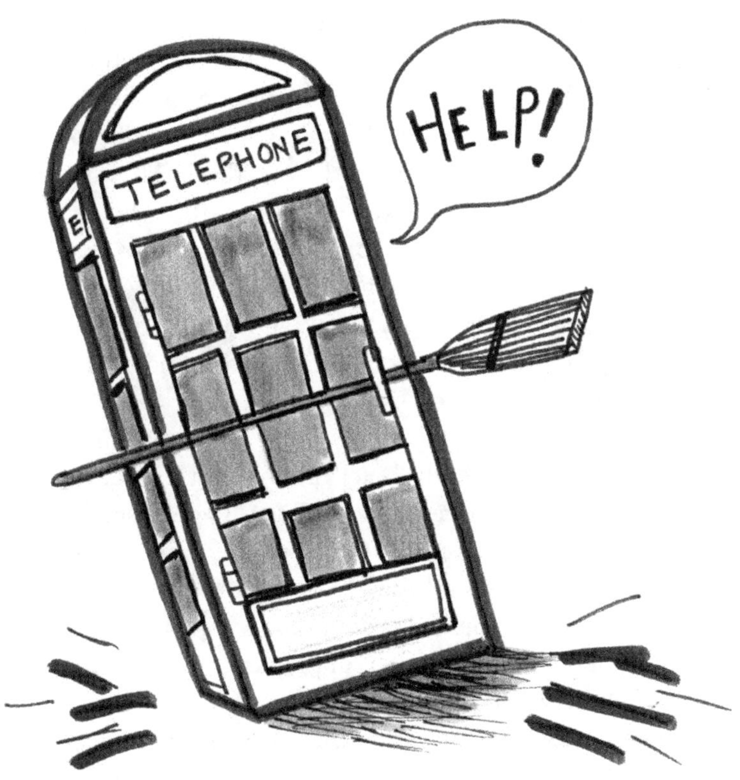
HELP!
TELEPHONE

Houdini came to town again as a successful vaudevillian. His escape act, by then, was getting him top billing across the country. Houdini's publicity performance in Kansas City included a short stint in the city jail. Stripped and searched from head to toe, he was bound in five sets of handcuffs and leg irons. With his mouth sealed so no hidden aid could be obtained from there, Houdini was thrust in a cell and locked in with a three-bond lock, guaranteed to be burglar proof. Eight minutes later, he emerged, free as a bird. The story might well end with a triumphant Houdini calling his agent in Chicago to give him news of the great success his performance in Kansas City created, but there was more.

Houdini was staying at the Savoy Hotel at Ninth and Central. He did enter the hotel's phone booth. The problem was, he had been recognized. Traveling salesman E.L. Williams couldn't resist the opportunity to pull a prank on the master showman. Williams stuck a broom through the handles of the phone booth doors and trapped the handcuff king inside. Houdini, caught unprepared, lacking the tools he often kept concealed on his person to effect his release during performances, was infuriated. Kicking the door and yelling for help, the master escape artist had met his match. The patrons let him out after a short period of heckling and fun at the entertainer's expense. The humbled Houdini sulked angrily away, unappreciative of how entertaining he had been to the boys at the Savoy.

Kansas City...Missouri

Folks who don't know the history of the Kansas City area find it confusing that the largest city in Missouri seems to be named after a neighboring state. The town of Kansas in Missouri was actually named after the Kansa, a Native American tribe that lived nearby. It predated the state of Kansas by over twenty-five years, during which time it grew into an important trade hub and outfitting town for travelers on the westward trails. In 1838, the Town of Kansas was formed; in 1853, the name was changed to the City of Kansas.

By the mid-1850s, the town was known as the City of Kansas and was subjected to intense pressure from both sides of the slavery debate, especially during the bloody years leading up to Kansas statehood. At that time, Missourian Mobillion McGee from Westport (now part of Kansas City), Missouri, suggested annexation of Kansas City into the Kansas territory. His reasoning was that it would bring a large number of proslavery voters into the mix and secure Kansas as a slave state. The scheme failed to gain enough support to come to a vote.

In 1879, Kansans, hoping to remove political and economic impediments to growth, pressed the Kansas legislature to pass a resolution to annex Kansas City, Missouri. The legislation passed, and as an incentive the plan offered to let Missouri keep the tax revenue from the city for a period of fifty years as compensation. The Missouri legislature rejected the annexation offer. In 1889, almost as an afterthought, the City of Kansas officially changed its name to Kansas City, Missouri.

West of the Kansas line were a number of communities, including the town of Wyandotte. Being just across the border from the larger community, the locals would say they were from Kansas City but then distinguish themselves from their near neighbor by adding "Kansas." In 1868, the Kansas City, Kansas Town Company was formed, and in 1872, Kansas City, Kansas, was incorporated.

It wasn't until 1881 that the governor of Kansas declared Kansas City, Kansas, a municipality of the second class (population more than two thousand and fewer than twenty-five thousand), and only with the 1886 incorporation of Armourdale, Kansas City and Wyandotte could Kansas City, Kansas, really call itself a city (Wyandotte was the largest of the three towns with a population of thirteen thousand).

Still, there were other attempts to annex Kansas City, Missouri, into Kansas again in 1884 and 1899 that also failed. In the meantime, the city of Kansas City, Kansas, annexed several smaller communities and became a growing force in the area. It is now the third-largest city in the state of Kansas and has experienced rapid economic growth in spite of a down economy.

Both cities have seen recent progress with the Legends shopping center, the Kansas City Speedway and Google choosing Kansas City, Kansas, to launch its Google Fiber Internet/television service, while Kansas City, Missouri, has added the Sprint Center, the Power and Light District and recently refurbished Royals and Chiefs stadiums.

With two large, successful Kansas Cities, one on each side of the state line, the confusion for visitors is likely to continue indefinitely, as neither side seems in any hurry to change its state of residence.

HURRAY, WE'RE NOT IN KANSAS ANYMORE

The Missouri River is so ornery that it's said that drinking its water is what gives the Missouri mule its attitude. During the steamboat era, the river claimed over four hundred steamships. The muddy water caked the insides of boilers, sometimes causing them to explode. The shifting current of the river snakes back and forth across broad valleys between high cliffs, jumping out and changing channels overnight, making it nearly impossible to travel the same route twice.

The forests along its banks provide fresh trees during flooding to pummel boats and create jams and hazards; some, known as sawyers, would catch bottom upside down and hide just below the surface. The roots and trunk would be held down most of the time by the current, but they could and would periodically bob up out of the muddy water and destroy a ship without ever being seen. In spring, it was flooding and ice floes from the upper river and in summer, sandbars and exposed trees. There was something new every season.

The biggest problem in the early days was that the river just wouldn't stay in one place. One engineer lamented, "I spent a year putting a bridge over the river; I've spent my time ever since keeping the river under the bridge." People living along the river learned to make the most of the situation; one joked that you never knew from year to year if you were going to harvest corn or catfish from the same plot of land.

In 1881, a great flood north of Kansas City shifted the channel from the Missouri side of the border to the Kansas side. Cow Island, formerly on the Kansas side, had a saloon on it owned by Charles Keane. After the flood, Keane was arrested and charged in Missouri for selling intoxicating liquor within the state's border. He was convicted at the circuit court in Platte City and then pleaded his case before the court of appeals in Kansas City.

The court ruled that since the river had changed course suddenly, rather than gradually, the former boundary would stand. The ruling was a boon to Keane, who could now legally sell his Kansas liquor to Missourians, without them having to take a ferry across the river. Cow Island is no longer an island; it also is no longer in Kansas. Both the river and the state line have shifted to the west of the site, and Kansas City Power and Light has a power plant there. No cows, saloons or catfish.

SKIN DIVER

The first Europeans to settle in the area of Kansas City were French trappers and fur traders. More specifically, François Chouteau and his wife, Berenice, sought to extend the Chouteau family's interests by building an outpost where the Kaw and Missouri Rivers came together. Before the Santa Fe trade, before the Oregon and California Trails, the fur trade drove men into the woods and rivers to seek their fortunes.

In March 1829, François Chouteau loaded a keelboat with over one thousand pelts—four hundred packages filled with beaver, otter, deer, raccoon, muskrat, wolf, badger and buffalo skins were jammed into the hold. François' brother, Frederick Chouteau, was put in charge of the ship. Bound for St. Louis, the boat also carried the widow of Barnett Vasquez (the first Indian agent to the Kaw tribe) and her children. Two Indian agents, two pilots, eight hands and ten Kaw Indians were also along for the ride. The pilot of the craft, Baptiste Datchurut, had been drunk and failed to show up at the appointed time. Frederick Chouteau hired another pilot, but before they made Independence, the old oarsman had obtained a canoe and caught up with the group. Datchurut took his post at the large steer oar and managed to steer the craft right into a large rock, knocking a hole in the deck.

Several of the men, including Chouteau, jumped off the sinking ship and swam for shore. Three drowned.

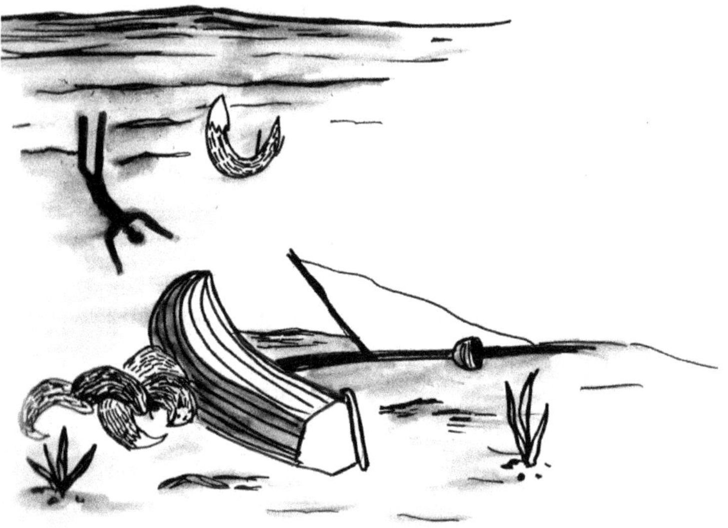

Chouteau made his way quickly to the nearest ferry and obtained a flatboat with which he rescued the rest of the people on board.

The next day, Chouteau and several of the men returned to the sunken boat to try and salvage what they could. They chopped a hole in the deck of the overturned ship and fished out a few packets near the opening, but the majority of the cargo was sunken out of sight in the murky water below. Then the cook for the outfit, a slave named Joseph Lulu, volunteered to make the dangerous descent into the ship. He returned with a pack of furs and then went under again. Diving over 375 times into the dark waters over the course of the day, Lulu saved all the furs. Joseph had saved the entire winter's income for the Chouteaus. To show his gratitude, Francois Chouteau freed Joseph Lulu. Joseph became a fireman on a steamboat but then was killed when it blew up just a few years later.

The life and death struggles, the unique attitudes about freedom and slavery and the all-or-nothing nature of business in Kansas City's early days shaped the fortunes of those who lived here then and helped create the character and personality of the town they built.

WHAT'S FOR BREAKFAST?

A little over one hundred years ago, kids in Kansas City might have eaten the new Post Grape Nuts or Kellogg's Corn Flakes for breakfast. But the drinks they washed them down with didn't include Sunny D or V-8. District officials became alarmed in 1910 when a sample survey of two classrooms indicated what students were drinking with their meals. In one classroom, five children indicated they had beer for breakfast, while twenty had drunk coffee. With each meal, the number of drinkers increased. At dinner, one classroom had nine beer drinkers and one each drinking wine or whiskey. In the

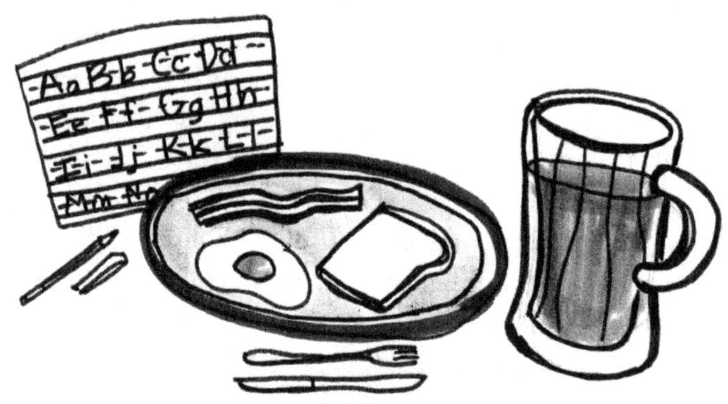

other classroom, fifteen of the kids had beer with dinner. School officials outlined a plan in response, hoping to send out nurses who speak the foreign languages necessary to train parents in proper nutrition, as children in "certain" neighborhoods were believed to be allowed free reign as to diet.

It was indicated that much of the nervousness among children in the district might be related to the drinking of stimulants and intoxicants. Well, that explains it—between the coffee and beer, it's no wonder kids in great grandpa's day were always able to stay awake in class and fall right to sleep at bedtime!

PARTY TOWN

I guess it isn't so surprising that some Kansas City kids had a drink every once in awhile. As early as June 1804, Kansas City began its career as a place to party. Lewis and Clark's Voyage of Discovery had paused at the Kaw's mouth for the night when two of the soldiers in the group got into the alcohol that was brought for the trip. John Collins simply passed out after his revels, but Hugh Hall took advantage of Collins's absence of consciousness to steal all the whiskey the group had. The two were severely punished. Hall received fifty lashes, and Collins (who was supposed to be guarding the supplies) received one hundred.

A few years later, the French community that was started by the Chouteaus was known for its celebrations, with music, dancing and occasional drinking. Gabriel Prudhomme, the owner of the landing and property that would become the town of Kansas, was killed in a tavern brawl involving several of the settlers in Chouteau's community. During the early years of settlement, alcohol continued to flow freely at Albert Boone's tavern (now Kelly's in Westport) and other trading posts and taverns in the Kansas City area. The Blue Goose Saloon stood somewhere on the hillside around where Third Street and Nebraska Avenue met. The front of the building was on level ground, but the rear had been built up on stilts.

One night, a posse was returning from a fruitless search for one of the outlaw bands that plagued the area. The call went out as the men neared town that a race was on—to the Blue Goose and up to the bar on horseback. The loser would be stuck with the bill. The mad dash brought horse and man inside the building; the bartender dutifully mixed drinks as the horses hung their heads over the bar. All at once, the floor gave, collapsing into a pile of horses, men, drinks, bartender, bar and posse all in a heap. Amazingly, no one was injured. A new Blue Goose was later built on level ground, with a floor reinforced to hold the occasional horse and rider.

The Civil War brought Federal troops into Kansas City and gave the local brewing industry a shot in the arm as enlisted men became regular customers at the local taverns. After the war, the rise in traffic on the westward trails, coupled with a growing economy based in cattle and agriculture, brought even larger numbers of saloonkeepers into Kansas City, including Jim Pendergast and his younger brother, Tom. At one point, Kansas City's first ward had the wettest block in the world, with twenty-three out of twenty-four businesses being saloons. Brewers in Kansas City were very competitive.

By 1899, the Heim brothers had the largest brewery in the world. They built a streetcar line from the downtown Market Square to their brewery in the East Bottoms in an effort to entice even more townspeople to come out for fresh beer. When the line failed to produce enough traffic, they built an amusement park near the brewery that brought in even more riders.

The Heim brothers' Electric Park had thousands of lights to illuminate its roller coaster, scenic railway, carousel, skating rink, swimming pool, bowling alley, alligator farm, dime museum, theaters, dance pavilion, penny arcade, shooting gallery, flower gardens, lake, bandstand and, of course, beer garden. There were nightly performances of costumed women dancing to an electric light show on a platform on a fountain in the lake. From 1899 until 1907, the park drew visitors to the brewery. A second park was built and stayed in business until the 1930s, by which time the Heim brothers' brewery was out of business—a victim of Prohibition.

Although the breweries were closed during Prohibition, Kansas City under boss Tom Pendergast stayed well supplied with liquor. As clubs in other cities dried up, Kansas City experienced a jazz renaissance. Performers like Charlie Parker, Count Basie and "Shouting Joe" Turner kept the party going all night long at clubs like Dante's Inferno, Hell's Kitchen, the Hi Hat and Hey, Hey. The repeal of Prohibition and later conviction of Boss Tom brought the booze business back out in the open, where anyone could get in on it.

In 1973, a new Kansas City party tradition began when radio personality Mike Murphy and two cohorts painted a calf green and paraded it outside their favorite watering hole on St. Patrick's Day, dubbing it "history's shortest and worst parade." Subsequent years brought bigger and bigger crowds and more participants until the most recent parade drew over 500,000 people and has become one of the nation's largest St. Patrick's Day celebrations. More recently, the opening of the Power and Light District, renewal of the Eighteenth and Vine jazz district and the rise of several microbreweries have kept the tippling tradition going in Kansas City.

Mind Your Own Business

Back in the 1890s, telephone technology was still in its infancy. In those days, an operator was required to make a connection for each call. That all changed when Almon Brown Strowger moved to Kansas City. Strowger had been a schoolteacher and served in the Union cavalry during the Civil War. At some point after the war, Strowger had taken up the trade of undertaker. It was his work, or rather lack of work, in that field that drove him to invention. It seems another undertaker in town was getting most of the business, and Strowger wasn't getting many calls.

Strowger found out that his competitor's wife was the local telephone operator, and when someone called wanting an undertaker, she would route the call to her husband. Strowger felt that the customer should be able

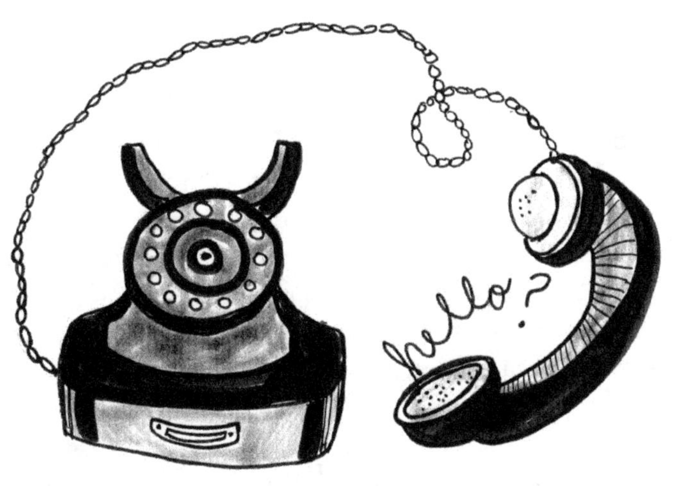
hello?

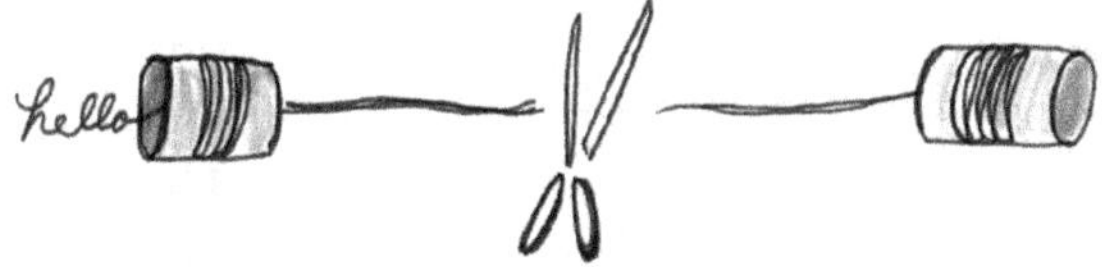
hello

to choose who was called without interference and set out to fix the problem. The result of his efforts was the automatic telephone exchange, which evolved into the rotary dial phone.

The switching system Strowger invented expanded the number of connections that could be made in a community and made it possible for the customer to complete the process without assistance. Rotary dial phones and operator-run switchboards are now museum pieces. But in March 1891, with his newly patented switching system, Strowger was sure people would be "dying" to give him more business, if they only had a chance.

Happy Pans

In the days before Marion Trozzolo came along, Americans spent thousands of hours a year scrubbing and scraping cooking pans. Marion was born in Castrolibro, Italy. His family immigrated to the United States when he was still a toddler, and he grew up in Chicago.

Trozzolo received a Silver Star and a Purple Heart for his military service in World War II. After the war, he received his bachelor's degree in philosophy and a master's degree in business administration from the University of Chicago. In 1951, he moved to Kansas City and began teaching business administration and economics at Rockhurst University. In

1957, he founded Laboratory Plasticware Fabricators and began work with Teflon as a coating for a magnetic stirring rod. In 1961, he introduced the first Teflon-coated pan in the United States: the "Happy Pan."

Trozzolo's Teflon-coated frying pans changed the way Americans cooked. Cleaning time and effort were greatly reduced for anyone using the new-style pan.

The nonstick frying pans were a huge hit, and Trozzolo became so associated with Teflon locally that he was asked to use the material to cover the fence around President Truman's home in Independence.

Now those tourist's messy handprints just wash right off.

Happy Meals

That's right, it started here. The bane of nutritionists and the joy of children across America had its debut in Kansas City. The McDonald's Happy Meal was first test marketed in Kansas City in October 1977. The idea had come from a franchise store in Argentina, the marketing plan was put together by Bernstein-Rein Advertising Company of Kansas City and the meal consisted of a hamburger, fries, cookies and a drink, along with a prize.

The first Happy Meal used a circus wagon theme for the box, and prizes included tops, McDonaldland character erasers, a McDoodle stenciler and identification bracelets. The meals were a hit locally and were introduced in McDonald's all across the country by 1979. Over 2.5 million Happy Meals are sold per day, and there have been literally billions of them sold worldwide, but they got their first thumbs up here in Kansas City.

Yeah, It's Got a Hemi!

Kansas City, with both Ford and General Motors assembly plants, has a long tradition of automobile manufacturing, longer than most Kansas Citians realize. As early as 1894, Baker and Elberg were building an electric car here. In 1901, there were only two cars in Kansas City. Oddly enough, they crashed into each other that year at Eleventh and Grand.

In 1908, the Stafford Motor Car Company began manufacturing in Kansas City, Missouri. The Stafford was advanced for its time; it had a four-cylinder, thirty-horsepower engine with a chain-driven overhead camshaft and a hemispherical combustion chamber. It could cruise up to sixty miles an hour. The car's namesake, Terry Stafford, had run a bicycle repair shop in Topeka and then became involved in automobile design and manufacture there. He worked as superintendant of the Smith Motor Car company in Topeka from 1901 until 1908. In 1908, Stafford began his own company in Kansas City and began

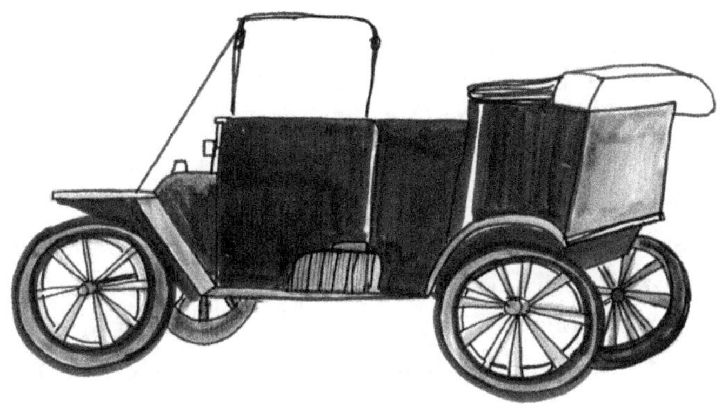

manufacturing the Stafford car, a five-seat open touring car with a buckle-down top.

Harry Truman was one of Stafford's Kansas City–area customers. He bought his 1911 Stafford used in 1915 for $600. He said, "It was an excellent car, and would take an awful beating." Truman drove the car for three years; he had it refitted into a hot roadster and took it with him to Camp Doniphan, then sold it for $200 before going overseas in 1918.

A new 1911 Stafford cost over $2,000, which was part of the problem Stafford faced. In 1909, Ford came out with the Model T, which sold new for around $800. Ford came to town that year with the opening of a factory in the Blue Valley Industrial District. The plant was near a source of raw materials, the Kansas City Nut and Bolt Steel Mill (later Sheffield and then Armco) and easy rail shipping to anywhere in the country.

In 1918, General Motors came to town and built the Fisher body factory and a Chevrolet plant in Leeds. Though Stafford made a good-quality automobile, less expensive mass-produced vehicles ultimately dominated the market. Stafford produced 314 cars between 1908 and 1915 before he dropped out of manufacturing and concentrated on repair work. (Stafford's company stayed in business until his death in 1925.)

There is only one remaining Stafford car in existence, now owned by a distant cousin to Terry, Denean Stafford. There is even evidence that leads Denean and family to believe that this last Stafford is, in fact, Harry Truman's old car. The vehicle has been restored and was displayed at the Kansas City Art Institute in 2009.

High Flyer

For many, the first airplane seen in the Kansas City area came in the form of a Wright brothers' Model EX piloted by Calbreath Perry Rodgers. Rodgers had taken only a ninety-minute lesson in flying at the Wright brothers' flying school before he passed his flying exam on August 7, 1911. He was the forty-ninth aviator to be certified to fly by the

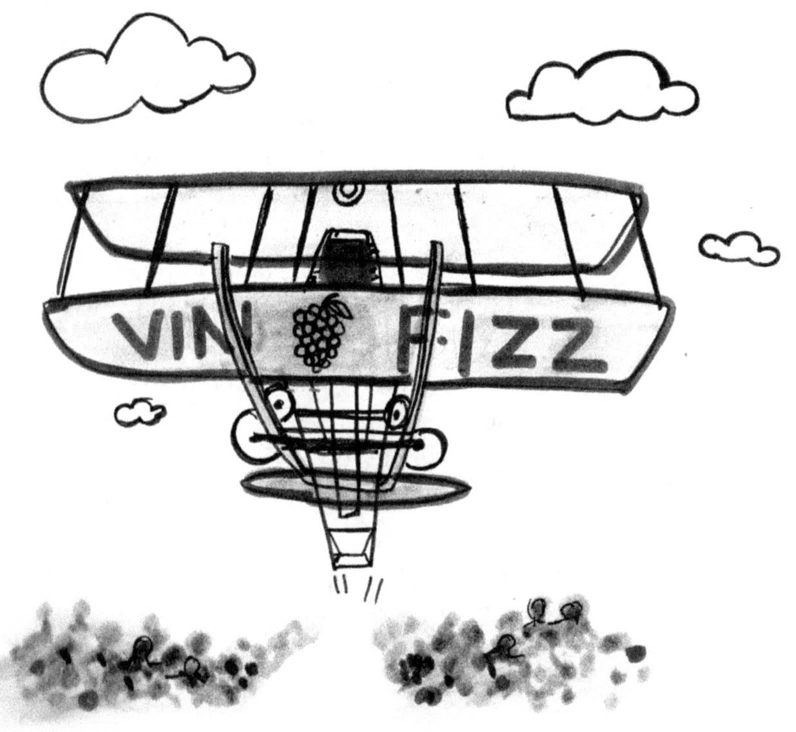

Federation Aeronautique Internationale and one of the first civilians to own a Wright flyer.

In October 1910, newspaper magnate Randolph Hearst had put up a prize of $50,000 for the first pilot to fly coast to coast in less than thirty days, and Rodgers, with little experience, attempted to make the trip in the fall of 1911. His plane was called the Vin Fizz, after a grape soft drink produced by the Armour Company. Armour had sponsored the flight by paying Rodgers around $5 for every mile he flew with an advertisement for Vin Fizz painted on the plane. Armour also provided a railroad hangar car with the Vin Fizz logo painted on it that carried Rodgers's family, support crew and spare parts for the plane. Rodgers's crew leader, Charles Taylor, was the chief mechanic for the Wright factory and had built the engine for the Wright brothers' first plane. A Piers Arrow automobile, which had the Vin Fizz logo painted on it as well, was brought along onboard the train to pick up Rodgers when the plane crashed or broke down away from the tracks (which it did several times).

Frequent delays had already made it clear that Rodgers would not win the Hearst prize on this trip; however, he had already made it much farther than the other two flyers who had made the attempt that year. As he neared the Kansas City area, excitement grew with the hope that this might be the first transcontinental flight to succeed. In Higginsville, people piled onto the roofs of nearly every business in town to see Rodgers, who circled twice over town.

In Odessa, whistles blew so people would know to come outside when the plane passed over. Rodgers landed in Blue Springs to make some minor repairs and then pushed on to Kansas City, where some schools were dismissed to see the historic flight. Rodgers had originally planned to follow the

Blue River South toward the park, but the urge to see the town from the air was too much, and Perry flew on west. Perry flew over the intersection of the Kaw and Missouri Rivers and then turned south, flying over a great deal of the city. He flew over the American Royal livestock show and thrilled the crowd there. He followed Grand Avenue south, where downtown pedestrians and office workers strained to catch a quick glimpse of the historic flight. Whistles blew in the packinghouses, sending thousands of workers out to see the "birdman." Lookouts from Jackson School at Twelfth and Ewing spotted Perry next and sent all 422 students streaming out into the schoolyard to cheer the flyer on. Finally, he headed southeast to the waiting reception committee at his original destination. Nearly 10,000 people were gathered in anticipation of Rodgers's arrival at Swope Park.

When the plane came within sight, the crowd mobbed the ropes. The plane circled down from two hundred to fifty feet overhead and then set down easily in the area cordoned off for it. As Rodgers landed, the crowd of well-wishers surged forward, brushing aside the mounted police and the motorcycle patrol in a rush to congratulate and shake the hand of the aviator. The Vin Fizz was grounded for two days in Kansas City due to bad weather, and then Rodgers continued his flight. Though Rodgers didn't win the Hearst prize, he did finish the trip, landing in Pasadena forty-nine days after leaving Sheepshead Bay in New York, being the first pilot to fly coast to coast.

Like many of the early aviation pioneers, Rodgers's passion was his downfall. A few months after completing his transcontinental trip, he was killed during a flying exhibition at Long Beach, California, in April 1912. He was the twenty-second American aviator to die in a plane crash and the first to do so as a result of a bird strike. His plane now hangs in the Barron Hilton Pioneers of Flight exhibition at the Smithsonian National Air and Space Museum. The green letters on the underside of the wings still advertise the extinct Vin Fizz, just like they did in Kansas City one hundred years ago.

Going to the Dogs

Mrs. Sarah A. Richart spent many years as a schoolteacher in Kansas City, Kansas. Her commitment to education went well beyond the walls of the local schoolhouse. As first president of the Federation of Clubs, Mrs. Richart was tasked with leading the group's efforts to develop a public library for Kansas City, Kansas.

The group had raised some funds, but its membership was too small to solely bear the cost. In a moment of inspiration, the former teacher found a way to solve the dilemma. In a meeting with Mayor R.L. Marshman, she suggested a plan: "The city is overrun with dogs that pay no license." Mrs. Richart then suggested, "I will collect the dog tax for one-half of it, and turn the other half into the treasury." The mayor liked the idea and asked, "What will we call you?" and she replied, "Call me the official dog enumerator." From that point forward, the plan took hold, and not just in Kansas City.

Word got out, and a number of communities across the country followed suit and began tapping Fido for the funds to fill their library shelves. For months, Mrs. Richart tirelessly worked to expand the list of licensed canines, and with the registration of each new poodle or mutt, she raised revenue for the city while increasing the library fund.

The industrialist Andrew Carnegie also made funds available for a building in Kansas City, Kansas, as he had elsewhere, and property was set aside for the project. But stocking the shelves was a different matter. It was the leadership of Mrs. Richart that brought the community together, man and beast, to raise funds to buy thousands of books needed for the library.

In 1903, shortly after Mrs. Richart's death, Kansas City, Kansas, opened its new library at Sixth and Minnesota, and today there are four other branch locations to serve the community. Pretty "doggone" good for one determined lady and man's best friend.

DROPPED CALLS?

It's often said that history repeats itself or there's nothing new under the sun. In 1909, Kansas City police chief W. W. Cook reported that a new plan to combat theft of copper phone line would be tried. Fast-forward one hundred years and again a rash of copper thefts has been reported in Kansas City, coincidental with a spike in the price of copper.

Besides the annoyance of loss of service for customers, the phone company is forced to spend time and money replacing the lost line—a lot of money. In Kansas City, Kansas, alone, AT&T reported the loss of over $10,000 worth of copper line within the first three months of 2012. Back in 1909, the phone company reported an equally large loss of one thousand pounds of copper phone line to thieves.

So what was the solution Chief Cook tried? Two English bloodhounds were engaged to track down and bring the thieves to justice. Nowadays, bloodhounds are used to search for lost pets, help find lost hikers and even to hunt down ivory poachers in Africa. Who knows, maybe a low-tech solution encouraged by a few doggie biscuits could save us all some money, prevent a few dropped calls and put these bad guys out of business.

Kansas City's First World Championship Team

In 1905, the first athletic team from Kansas City to win a World Championship won the championship game at home. The game wasn't football or baseball, and there was no official organization to convey the title, but the Kansas City team did beat the most well-known and, up to that point, undefeated team in the new sport of basketball.

In 1891, James Naismith invented the game, and by 1895, he was in Independence, Missouri, organizing the first team there. By 1905, basketball was being played all over the country, and the Kansas City Athletic Club had organized a team called the Blue Diamonds. Naismith had moved on to become the first basketball coach for the University of Kansas (KU), where he was trying to establish a winning tradition (although KU lost to the Blue Diamonds in its first season, 1898–1899, and Naismith was the only coach in the team's history to have a losing record.)

The Blue Diamonds were a good amateur team, and they wanted a shot at beating the best. In 1904, the team from Buffalo, New York, had won the Amateur Athletic Union National Championship at the World Fair held in St. Louis and was declared the world champion of the game. In 1905, the Buffalo team agreed to play the Blue Diamonds at the Kansas City convention hall. The Blue

Diamonds had been fortunate to have a group of brothers from Independence who were exceptional players. One of the brothers, Forrest "Phog" Allen, doubled as guard and team manager, both playing in and scheduling the contest.

Three games were played. The first had around 1,200 people attend. The *Kansas City Star* covered the game, praising the ability of the Buffalo team. Buffalo won by four points, but Buffalo had brought its own referee, and in a close game, several calls were contested, as was the final score. A second game was played using a local referee with similar complaints; Buffalo lost its first game ever. The third and final match was held on March 29, 1905, and had an attendance of 5,000 fans. A neutral referee who was an expert on the rules of the game was found. University of Kansas athletic director, the man who wrote the rules of the game, James Naismith, judged the contest. The Blue Diamonds won 45–14 and became the world champions. Forrest Allen ended up playing three years at KU for Naismith and eventually took over as head coach there. Allen racked up nearly six hundred wins as head coach of the Jayhawks over thirty-nine seasons, winning twenty-four conference championships and three national championships. He is considered the "Father of Basketball Coaching," having helped organize the National Association of Basketball Coaches and serving as its first president. He was also inducted into the first class of the Basketball Hall of Fame and received an Olympic gold medal in 1952 as coach of the winning U.S. team. The basketball arena at the University of Kansas is named Allen Field House in his honor.

The Blue Diamonds are no more, and these days Kansas City has no NBA franchise and is not known as a basketball town. But a little over one hundred years ago, Kansas Citians could honestly claim that they had the world's best team, the world's best coach and the world's most qualified referee all together in one game—and their team won.

Hatchetator

During the Civil War, she was forced to move to Kansas City. At the turn of the century, she was told by a judge to leave the town and never come back. Her first husband died of alcoholism. Her second husband divorced her because of her crusade against alcoholism. Her daughter died an alcoholic as well. She was alternately thrown in jail or threatened with violence and then lauded for her efforts and paid to give lectures. She was considered a moral crusader by some and a crackpot by others. She sold miniature axes to raise funds for her efforts, mirroring her weapon of choice when she went saloon busting.

Carrie Nation fought the scourge of alcoholism with all her might for twenty years. She championed moral living, assailing alcohol and tobacco for the damage they did to

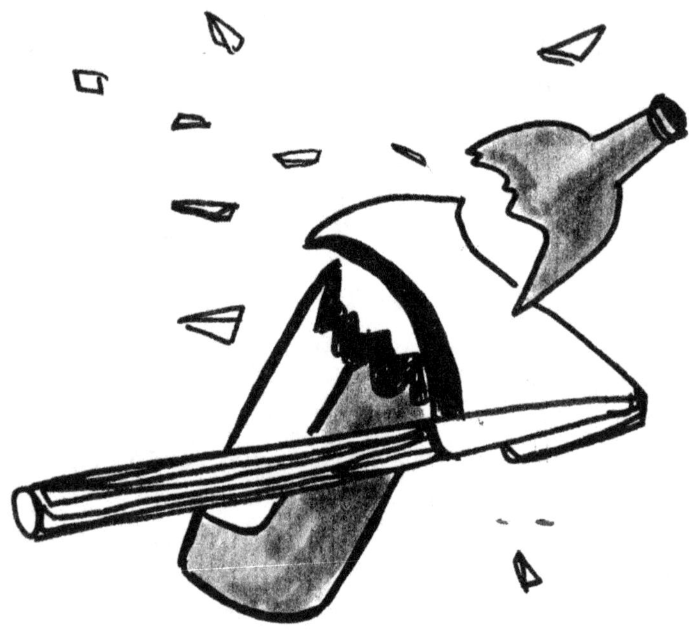

families. Taking the fight to the enemy, the six-foot-tall Nation would enter a saloon and start smashing liquor bottles and furniture. She used rocks early on but found the hatchet was better for throwing at glassware, and it became a symbol of her struggle against the demon rum.

In 1901, she entered a number of establishments around Twelfth Street in Kansas City. She was arrested and faced a fine of $500 (no small sum in those days), but the judge said the fine would be imposed only if she ever came back to Kansas City. With money raised in part by the sale of her souvenir hatchets, Carrie purchased a twenty-three-room brick home in Kansas City, Kansas, at Reynolds and Grandview Avenues. She intended it to be a home for women whose husbands or fathers were alcoholics.

The home for drunkards' wives and mothers was given to associated charities to run, but few alcoholics' wives showed up, and the house ended up being used to house single mothers mostly. Nation's crusade led to speaking engagements in the East but declined into vaudeville, where she finally was performing as part of the sideshow at Coney Island. She died in 1911 of an apparent heart attack. She was buried in an unmarked grave in what is now the Kansas City suburb of Belton, Missouri.

Strange Bedfellows

Politics make strange bedfellows, but these guys brought their own sheets. In 1924, Kansas City hosted the national Klonvocation of the Ku Klux Klan. Though the Klan had been around since Reconstruction, it had waxed and waned in power.

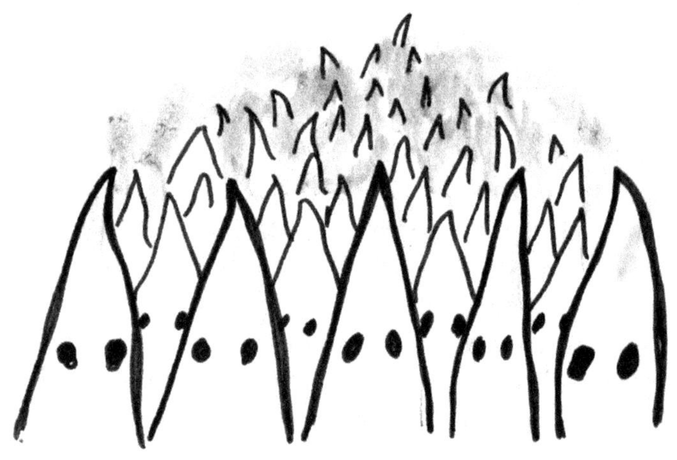

Operating as a secret society, often prone to violence and intimidation in order to maintain white political and cultural dominance, the Klan started and was strongest in the South, although there were adherents to the group's segregationist, anti-Catholic, anti-Jewish, anti-immigrant message in other parts of the country as well. The original Klan had many Confederate veterans as members. A former general, Nathan Bedford Forrest, was believed to be a leader, if not the Grand Wizard, of the group. Infighting and rising violence caused Forrest to officially disband the group in 1869, but there continued to be local incarnations ever since.

In 1915, the D.W. Griffith movie *Birth of a Nation* presented a heroic image of the Klan defending white society from out-of-control blacks and Northern carpetbaggers. The film was widely popular and would be used for the next fifty years by the group as a recruiting tool. *Birth of a Nation* was the highest-grossing film of 1915, and its continued sales kept it at the spot until another revisionist film about the old South, *Gone with the Wind*, surpassed it twenty-four years later. The film brought about a rebirth of the Klan as a national organization, with massive numbers of new recruits from all over the country.

The group began actively recruiting members in the early '20s, with sales- and publicity-driven leadership. By 1922, it was taking in $35,000 per day. The new Klan made efforts to team up with other groups intent on moral reform. The Women's Christian Temperance Union (WCTU) had been around since the 1870s, and prohibition and women's rights topped its agenda. The "new" Klan was for prohibition and white women having the franchise; it contributed money to the WCTU. By tailoring its message to fit the concerns of potential allies, the Klan further extended its reach, partnering with more mainstream Christian groups.

By 1924, when the Klan came to Kansas City, the organization had three million members and immense political leverage, which it used on both parties but especially within the Democratic Party. The response to the rise of the Klan varied widely on both sides of the state line. Journalist William Allen White was so appalled at the rise of the Klan's influence on both parties in Kansas that he ran as an independent candidate for governor.

Jackson County judge Harry Truman was pressured to join the Klan in 1924 but claimed that after a meeting where he was asked to promise not to hire Catholics in his administration he quit and asked for a refund of his dues.

In Independence, Liberty and Lee's Summit, thousands joined the organization, while in Kansas efforts were made to oust the organization from the state. A 1922 meeting of the Klan in Kansas City saw twenty thousand attendees. By partnering with less radical groups, the Klan made massive inroads into mainstream politics. The Democratic National Convention of 1924 (sometimes called the Klanbake) was disrupted as the group tried to exert its influence on the national stage.

The secret society successfully opposed the nomination of Al Smith (a Catholic) but was unable to force the convention to accept its candidate: William Gibbs McAdoo. The Democrats settled on compromise candidate John W. Davis, who was then defeated by President Coolidge. The fall of the new Klan's popular influence was as gradual as its rise was rapid. No one event precipitated the change; rather, a slow awakening of conscience whittled away mainstream support to the point where it's now hard to believe that so many ordinary people in Kansas City fell under its sway.

Second Best

He was a hard worker who kept falling short of his dreams. In 1915, he was the second-best Charlie Chaplin impersonator in Kansas City. He had entered several Chaplin impersonation contests (mostly sponsored by local theaters) and won a bit of money at it. He even received an offer to perform in vaudeville, but an accidental injury to his foot left him unable to accept. Before that, he had attempted and failed to learn to play the violin. He tried to get a job at the *Kansas City Star* but was turned down, though he had worked on his father's *Star* route delivering papers. He was a dreamer who had spent a summer traveling, but failing to sell magazines, on trains, actually owing money to his supplier by the time he quit. During World War I, he wanted to join the army but was turned down. He then volunteered as a Red Cross ambulance driver but caught the flu and arrived too late for the war.

Returning to Kansas City in 1919, he lived for a while in his brother's garage. He got a job as a commercial artist at an advertising agency but was fired within a month for his lack of drawing ability. He started his own business but lost most of his employees because he couldn't afford to pay them. He finally was living in his office, subsisting on charity from a nearby restaurant. At one point, he was stranded at home because he had left his shoes to be repaired at a shop in his building, and he couldn't afford to pay the $1.50 repair fee. His business was a failure.

He took the last bit of money he had to buy a ticket to Los Angeles, stopping in a lot to open a box and evict his former roommate—a pet mouse. Walt Disney left Kansas City just ahead of bankruptcy proceedings against his failed Laugh-a-gram Studio.

He took with him the hard experiences of his many failures here and made one more try in California. Using footage from a project he had started in Kansas City, Disney got his new start with a distribution deal for his live action/cartoon Alice series, which featured Kansas City native Virginia Davis in the role of Alice (at least for the first fourteen films in the series of fifty-seven). Finally, he began to gain some traction, and with the 1928 debut of *Steamboat Willie*, Disney achieved universal acclaim. Walt had started hiring back his old gang from his unsuccessful business in Kansas City as soon as the Alice series got going. Ub Iwerks, Isadore "Fritz" Freleng, Rudolph Ising, Hugh Harman and Joseph Benson "Bugs" Hardaway all ended up making their way out West and were involved in creating some of the most successful and memorable cartoon characters and series in history. Walt's Kansas City cadre not only helped bring Disney's ideas to the screen but also gave Pink Panther, Porky Pig, Yosemite Sam, Tweety Bird and Sylvester, Merry Melodies, Looney Tunes and a host of others to the world. Walt made millions. The Kansas City boys all had great successes of their own, and vaudeville struggled on a few more years, minus one Charlie Chaplin impersonator.

LOST TREASURE

In the fall of 1864, an invading army of Confederate soldiers was coming to Kansas City. Thousands of men, vastly outnumbering the citizens of town, were sweeping across the state of Missouri. The telegraph lines had been cut, rail travel had been interrupted and rumors outnumbered facts. Kansas politicians had said the Confederates wouldn't come, had even ridiculed the whole idea. Kansas's Governor Carney had reluctantly called for militia to form on the border. Samuel R. Curtis, the Union general in charge of the border, reinforced the governor's call to arms by declaring martial law in Kansas and requiring all able-bodied men between eighteen and sixty to report for duty. Kansas Citians feared the worst as Price advanced through Lexington and forced Curtis back from Independence. A trickle and then a stream of townspeople came to the door of Father Bernard Donnelley. Each of them brought money or other valuables, hoping the priest might hide them in case the invading army should succeed in taking the town.

Donnelley gathered the goods, put them in a large wooden box and, with the help of a sexton, buried it in

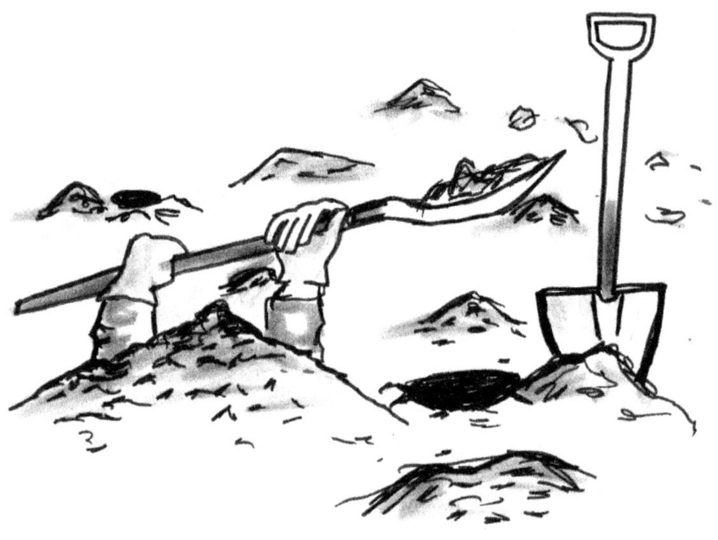

an old cemetery near the church. Concerned that the man who helped him do the burying might let slip where the valuables were located, the priest went out and dug up the box and moved it. Again, fearing he might have been seen, Donnelley dug up and reburied the loot a third time.

During the battle, Father Donnelley fearlessly joined the army at the front, treating the wounded, loading ambulances, giving last rites and even burying the dead. He spent the next several weeks helping at hospitals and homes where the throngs of wounded men were being tended. When Father Donnelley finally returned to dig up the valuables he had been entrusted with, he could not find the spot where he had placed them. He had paced off the distance and dug where he thought the box should be but found nothing. Fruitless weeks of searching produced nothing. Father Donnelley took out a loan against property he owned and paid back all who had entrusted him with their valuables.

The priest searched unsuccessfully for years, hoping to find his lost treasure, even leaving his sickbed the week he passed away to search one more time. The old cemetery fell out of use and was nearly forgotten until 1986, when road grading equipment being used near Twelfth Street and Pennsylvania Avenue turned up skeletal remains and reignited the quest for the priest's lost treasure. Though nothing was found at that time, locals still occasionally speculate and even occasionally go searching for Father Donnelley's lost loot from the 1860s.

Throwing Rotten Eggs in Frog Eye

Kansas City, being situated on the "muddy" Missouri River, isn't well known for its mineral baths and healing waters, but it once was. In fact, at one time the mineral springs at Frog Eye were such a draw that thousands of health seekers would come there to buy barrels of water and toss a rotten egg or two at a man with his head sticking through a board.

The guy with egg on his face was just one of the many vendors trying to make a quick buck from the tourists at Frog Eye, Missouri (later renamed Mineral City). In addition to concession stands, there was a rodeo, a bowling alley, a baseball field and a dunk tank to entertain the tourists who came to camp and sample the waters on well-owner Steve Mullen's land. Although not in Kansas City proper, Frog Eye was just one of several surrounding communities that became popular for their mineral springs.

Even though Kansas City had a few springs of its own (Young's Medical Well at Twenty-fifth and Vine, Magneso-Saline Mineral Spring at Kensington and Cincinnati, Twin Springs at 3500 Independence Avenue and Union Spring on East Sixth Street), the smaller outlying communities had more luck at attracting health seekers and tourists.

Excelsior Springs, northeast of Kansas City, was one of the most popular destinations in the state at one time, its multiple springs drawing as many as 350,000 tourists a year during the Roaring Twenties. The Elms Hotel in Excelsior Springs catered to the more discriminating customer. Al Capone stayed there and played poker all night, and President Harry Truman celebrated his 1948 election there with a mineral bath.

In Liberty, Missouri, there was a resort hotel at Reed Springs.

Independence had several public springs that had, in fact, dictated the location and platting of the town. The many springs were a boon to locals and travelers on the several trails west that started there. One such spring, Vaile Spring, flowed near the Harvey Vaile mansion (later used as a sanitarium and today a historic house museum) and its water was bottled and sold as a tonic and fortifier.

North of Kansas City, Peerless Spring lies under Smithville Lake, as does Plattsburg Mineral Spring (a once popular resort).

In Johnson County, Missouri, Pertle Springs drew crowds in the thousands, and William Jennings Bryant and Carrie Nation were featured speakers at the giant assembly hall built there.

There were sulfur springs, magnetic springs, saline springs and even radium springs, each with its own healing powers. The springs' downfall was the development of new methods of dealing with illness. The rise of antibiotics, Salk's polio vaccine, et cetera, just proved more reliable than spa treatments. By the 1960s, most insurance companies stopped paying for therapeutic mineral baths, and the resorts that had survived the lean Depression and war years began closing their doors. Where dozens of resorts once populated the Kansas City area, only Excelsior Springs remains, the Elms still serving a much-diminished group of tourists who still seek the healing waters near the city of fountains.

Stampede

On July 24, 1928, the rodeo came to town, but it came without notice. It started with a train pulling out of Union Station, hauling several cars with cattle on board. A few blocks away, the train derailed. Eleven of the animals were killed in the pileup that followed, but 139 terrified beasts dashed away from the wreckage into the streets of the city.

One animal found his way into the women's restroom at Union Station. An employee there managed to wrestle the steer down on the slick floor and then tie it to a post in the building until it could be retrieved. Another animal crashed through the front window of a parking garage, damaged several cars inside and then smashed through another window in the back of the building. As if this weren't enough to tax the night shift at the police station, in another unrelated incident the same night at Thirty-ninth Street, a truckload of hogs was overturned, and forty pigs had to be corralled as well.

By 1928, there were lots of automobiles in Kansas City, and a thousand-pound steer could do a lot of damage to those early machines. Cowboys were brought in and tried to rope the confused steers; more than once, their loops missed and caught on the fenders of cars as the beasts weaved in and out of downtown traffic. Motorists found themselves competing for space with the cattle, and more than a few cars were gored. Reports came in all over town. Two squad

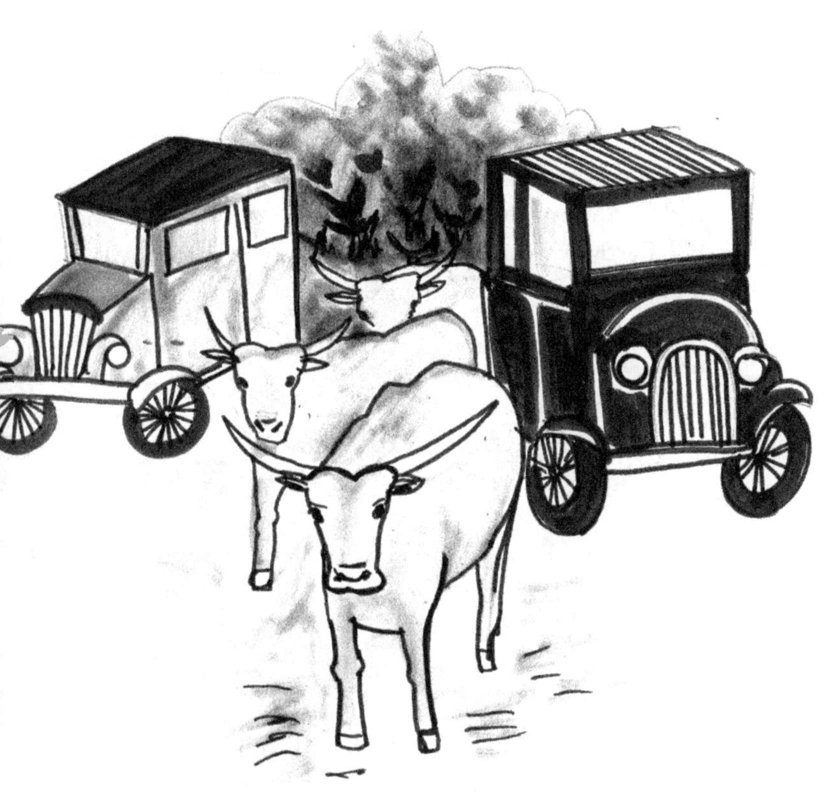

cars faced off a group of five steers in Penn Valley Park. The leader of the group turned suddenly and stepped on the running board of one of the cars. Sticking his head in the window, he bellowed at the policemen, and the car stalled out. He then led his crew away onto Broadway.

The roundup took two days, as miniature rodeos broke out throughout downtown and into the neighborhoods. Small herds were gathered to be returned to the rails, and eventually the cow town was able to resume being a busy metropolis.

Kansas City Mules

Mules helped build Kansas City. The first year after Missouri attained statehood, William Becknell used mules from Mexico to haul goods and open commerce along the Santa Fe Trail. The resulting overland trade that developed was pivotal to the rise of the Kansas City area as a center of commerce. Independence and Westport became the jumping-off points for trails west, first to Santa Fe and then to Colorado, California and Oregon. The outfitting business, which included raising and supplying mules for the Santa Fe trade, built the fortunes of many of Kansas City's first families.

As many as 1,300 mules at a time would be driven through Independence, as the animal became a favorite for both traders and farmers. Farmers used mules as muscle to plow fields and haul produce; the army used mules as pack animals and sometimes as mounts in hill country, where they were considered more sure-footed than horses. (The U.S. Marine Corps used mules in operations in the mountains of Afghanistan as recently as 2012.)

The crack of the muleskinner's whip was a common sound in Independence and Westport as large teams brought wealth to the area from across the desert. In honor of the many unsung mules who contributed to the growth of the town, I want to offer these stories of two mules from the Kansas City area.

A mule named Sam saved the fortunes of two of Kansas City's early settlers. In the 1850s, Upton Hays and John Campbell were working for the outfitting team of Russell, Majors and Waddell. The two men were near Bent's Fort, nearly six hundred miles from Kansas City, when a stagecoach heading west passed them the news that the company was bankrupt. The two men held bonds worth thousands of dollars that would become worthless the minute the news got to Kansas City. Telegraph wire had not been strung from coast to coast at that point, so news traveled by stage. The men knew their financial success or ruin depended on beating that stage.

Hays set out immediately riding a mule named Sam. Hays and Sam couldn't outrun the teams of horses that would be switched for fresh mounts every 110 miles. Their only chance was to make up time by not stopping.

By sheer stubbornness and endurance they might be able to pull ahead over the course of several days. On the sixth day of their chase, the stage came into sight, and by the next day, Sam and Upton had pulled ahead. The exhausted mule and rider beat the stage to town. Hays stumbled into Kansas City and asked for cash. The clerk was reluctant at first, but as all the paperwork was in order, he delivered the cash to Hays, who walked out the door only moments before the stage pulled in. After securing the funds, Upton Hays slept for two days. Sam was rewarded for his efforts with an easy retirement and was never put to work again.

A short distance south of Kansas City is the town of Drexel, Missouri, hometown of arguably the most famous mule in history. Francis the Talking Mule was played by a mule named Molly from the Ed Frazier farm near Drexel. Frazier's farm had already provided Hollywood with a mule named Champ Clark to play Samson in the 1939 movie *I Am from Missouri* with actor Bob Burns. Burns liked Champ so much that he bought him after the movie was over. Hollywood's next Missouri Mule, Molly, was purchased for $200 and flown to Hollywood at an expense of $450. She was given a screen test and competed with eight other mules from across the United States for the role. She won the part with her personality, long eyelashes and photogenic face. The character Molly played was supposed to be male and able to talk. The deep and gravelly voice of Francis had a western twang and was provided by veteran character actor Chill Wills. There were seven Francis movies made in the 1950s, grossing Universal Studios millions of dollars. Molly got to work with stars Donald O'Connor and Mickey Rooney as her leads. Not bad for a country girl.

Hearts of Gold

The bawdy houses and red-light districts of many towns are often treated as family secrets. Everyone knows about them, but they just don't talk about it. The rough-and-tumble Old West towns were made up mostly of single men who worked hard and played hard at dangerous and dirty jobs.

Cowboys, ranch hands, miners, trappers, railroad crews, muleskinners and farmers usually came to towns like Kansas City with the intention of letting off some steam. Saloons and houses of prostitution thrived in these towns when they were young and unsettled. As communities became more permanent and wealthy and middle-class families put down roots, there was steady pressure to sweep such places under the rug.

The railroad and meatpacking industry combined to explode Kansas City's population in the late nineteenth century. The first year the railroad came to Kansas City (1869), it brought seventy thousand people there. By 1880, Kansas City was selling one million head of cattle a year, and the railroads were transporting thousands of them to markets.

The railroad men carried red signal lanterns with them, and the red lights would be left on the porches of the many saloons and bawdy houses these men frequented. Police limited the parts of town where such businesses were allowed to thrive, and they were called red-light districts.

The red-light district in Kansas City was near the Missouri River levee and close to the tracks, where the Pendergast political machine ruled and was given a percentage of the take. The boundaries were Second Street on the north, Main Street to the east, Sixth Street on the south and May Street on the west. By 1910, this area had 128 brothels that had made the Kansas City police fine list.

There was Clara's Crib at 1801 Main, the Hotel Ester at 2035 Broadway, the Irish Village at 1711 Walnut, Mollie Paupaw's on West Fourth, Bessie Stevenson's on Broadway, Mollie O'Brien's at First and Main, Em Williams's on Third Street and even a tent run by Becky Ragan at the foot of Main.

But there were three businesses next to one another that were the leading houses of the district: Madame Lovejoy's at 200 and 202 West Fourth, Eva Prince's Resort at 204 and 206 West Fourth and Annie Chambers's at the southwest corner of Third and Wyandotte (just north of Madame Lovejoy's).

These three businesses thrived for years in downtown Kansas City, while a blind eye was turned by the police and local government. The first-tier houses, like Annie Chambers's place, were well maintained and richly decorated. Chambers saw to it that her girls were well dressed and presented themselves in as positive a light as possible for the clients. The business was as well run as any male-dominated company in Kansas City.

The end of the big bawdy houses began with a wave of reform that started in the 1910s, broke most of the houses in the early 1920s and peaked with the sale of Madame Lovejoy's to Frank Ennis, who rented the house to Reverend and Mrs. David Bulkley, who in turn renamed it City Union Mission. The couple began doing missionary work in the neighborhood, providing help for men who battled alcoholism or had been recently released from prison. The reformers befriended several of the girls who worked in the two remaining houses. One of the girls who worked at Eva Prince's lost a child and asked Reverend Bulkley to perform the funeral service at the mission. Moved by the sermon and its effect on the girls who attended the funeral, Eva Prince decided to lease her house to the Bulkleys and eventually sold it to them, expanding the mission further.

Annie Chambers also heard the sermon over the lost child and had become friends with the Bulkleys as well. She decided to leave her home to the Bulkleys. Though she was retired and had given the house to the mission to use, Annie Chambers continued to live there and give testimony to visitors about her life as a madam. When Chambers passed away at the age of ninety-three, the last of the three houses joined the other two in becoming the City Union Mission, a Christian outreach organization that has served Kansas

City's poor for decades. The mission found its place in the heart of the city due in part to Kansas City's ladies of the night and their hearts of gold.

Kansas City Shuffle

It's a blindfold kickback type of a game
Called the Kansas City Shuffle
Whereas you look left and they fall right
Into the Kansas City Shuffle
It's a they-think you-think they don't know
Type of Kansas City hustle
Where you take your time
Wait your turn
And hang them, up and out to dry

Long before Bennie Moten recorded the song that associated Kansas City with a con game, the con men were busily fleecing the many marks who came in the waves of immigration and settlement that passed through town.

The Kansas City shuffle is a con where you let the sucker think he knows how a game or con is rigged and let his arrogance or ego lead him to bet heavily right before you switch the method of cheating. In *Forty Years a Gambler on the Mississippi*, George Devol tells of his adventures as a gambler and con man. He visited Kansas City in its infancy and tells how "at that time there were three or four houses and a hotel down at the river bank," and "I became acquainted with a man named McGee, who owned the largest part of Kansas City." The gambler and McGee played a game called "Seven Up" for ten dollars per game.

Devol claimed to have won five lots from McGee that he later sold for $10 each. One of Devol's partners was an odd-looking con by the name of Canada Bill. Bill cultivated the look of a rube and built his customers' confidence by seeming to be what he would ultimately make them: a victim. A compulsive gambler, one time Bill was losing at cards, and George told him the game he was in was fixed. Bill made the now-famous reply, "I know, George, but it's the only game in town." George claimed the team made over $200,000 in Kansas City before splitting up.

In the early 1870s, Bill made a killing throwing three-card monte and playing other cons on travelers on Union Pacific's Kansas City–Omaha line. The railroad received so many complaints that an attempt was made to ban Bill and other gamblers from the trains. Bill boldly responded by writing to the director of the Union Pacific Railroad offering an annual fee of $25,000 for exclusive rights to continue working the trains. As part of his offer, he promised to only prey on Chicago–Kansas City commercial travelers and Methodist ministers. He was turned down.

One of the most successful con men in history was known as Titanic Thompson. "Ti" worked in a number of states, including Missouri. Thompson was an excellent golfer, pool hustler, gambler and con man. He was the master of the proposition bet. One time, while in Kansas City, Thompson bet a group of high rollers that he could throw a pumpkin onto the roof of the ten-story-high Dixon Hotel on Baltimore Street. The bet was made, and Thompson produced a pumpkin the size of a baseball and threw it to the roof. Not being satisfied with the single con, Thompson offered double or nothing that he could throw a second pumpkin clear over the hotel, which occupied a full city block.

The marks fell for the shuffle, betting Thompson again and losing again. How he did it, one could guess: adding a lead weight to the center of the second pumpkin (he had done that with a peanut to make spectacular throws before), having a confederate on the roof to catch and finish the throw or perhaps planting a similar pumpkin on the other side of the building. Or, finally, he may have just practiced throwing midget pumpkins for days before, figured out the maximum distance he could throw and matched the building to his skill.

One thing's for sure, though: Thompson had the con all figured out ahead of time, including the second bet and how to make it irresistible to his marks.

Confederate Victory

In the 1960s television show *The Beverly Hillbillies* episode "The South Rides Again," Granny and the Clampett clan, unaware that the North won the War Between the States, defend Beverly Hills, successfully capturing Union general Ulysses S. Grant (a surprised reenactor from a movie shoot).

Paul Henning, who hailed from Jackson County, Missouri, was the creator of *The Beverly Hillbillies*. Henning grew up in Independence, where he may have gotten the ideas for many of his characters.

Before the Civil War, Jackson County was the home of the largest slave owner in the state of Missouri. The majority of its wealthy landowners, politicians and businessmen either owned slaves or benefitted financially from slavery. During the Civil War, guerrillas like William Quantrill and George Todd frequented its towns and were openly supported by much of the citizenry. It supplied the Confederate armies and Missouri State Guard with thousands of men. Union forces placed the county under martial law for years and still had to bring in more troops to enforce the peace after the rest of the Confederacy had surrendered.

Though downtown Kansas City had a Federal garrison and a sizeable pro-Union population, Westport and many of the surrounding towns had a majority who supported the Confederacy and slavery. Hundreds of diehards from Missouri under General Sterling Price and General Jo Shelby retreated into Mexico, burying their flag in the Rio Grande rather than surrender it or themselves to the Federal troops. Many of these unrepentant Confederates would return to the Kansas City area and regain social and even political standing to the extent that ex-Confederates were probably as powerful a political force, if not more so, than they had been before the war.

Their story was rarely told out loud, as it had to do with a family fight, and there's no reason to bring up the unpleasant past. However, the history of Kansas City, and of Missouri, was shaped for decades by men who had taken up arms in open rebellion against the government of the United States of America. Men who had come to Kansas City in 1864 with cannon and rifle and dark intentions somehow returned to become pillars of society.

Among these men was Major General John S. Marmaduke, Confederate States of America (CSA). Marmaduke commanded a division during Price's Raid, doing untold damage in Missouri and Kansas, especially around Kansas City, yet he was elected governor of the state of Missouri in 1884. Marmaduke was unrepentant during the campaign, appealing to former Confederates and their supporters to oust the carpetbagger Republicans. Confederate general Jo Shelby led raid after raid in Missouri and Arkansas. After Appomattox, he refused to surrender his forces, seeking a separate peace for two more years in Mexico, yet in 1893, he was appointed federal marshal for the Western District of Missouri and continued in that position for the rest of his life.

Sam Chiles served with Jo Shelby, went to Mexico, came back and was elected Jackson County marshal in 1898. He later moved to Buckner (just east of Independence) and served as an officer of the savings and loan there. He lived to the ripe old age of eighty-four and was considered a pillar of the community. My mother-in-law grew up in Buckner and knew Chiles as a child. On drives to her old hometown, she would point out his fine stone home, which still stands at the corner of 24 Highway and Buckner-Tarsney Road, across from the elementary school, and recall the exceptionally large number of people who attended his funeral and how well regarded he was.

John Newman Edwards served as adjutant to General Shelby throughout the Civil War. He was Shelby's biographer. After the war, he was a tireless defender of those who participated in the Lost Cause. As editor of the *Kansas City Times*, he decried the treatment, both during and after the war, of ex-guerrillas like Frank and Jesse James, comparing them to modern-day Robin Hoods. His paper gave voice to the many who had suffered under martial law in the Kansas City area and built up a mythology that entered the national consciousness. Jesse James won his war.

Hiram Bledsoe served in the Mexican-American War, helping capture a cannon at Sacramento. The Missourians kept "Old Sac," the cannon that had been cast from a church bell and had a distinctive "ring" when it was fired. At the start of the Civil War, Bledsoe joined the Missouri State Guard and brought Old Sac with him. He saw action at Lexington, Carthage, Wilson's Creek and Pea Ridge and then joined the regular Confederate army and fought at Vicksburg, Atlanta, Nashville and Chickamauga. He was wounded six times, ending the war at the rank of colonel and as chief of artillery, commanding twelve guns (plus Old Sac). Still, Bledsoe returned to Missouri, settled in Pleasant Hill (southeast of Kansas City), served several terms on the Cass County Court, became county collector and was even elected to the Missouri state senate.

President Harry Truman had two uncles and several cousins who fought for the Confederacy, even with Quantrill's guerrillas. He grew up in a Jackson County that was dominated by the Democratic Party, and much of it was unapologetic for its Confederate leanings. Truman's own mother rejected the idea of sleeping in the Lincoln Bedroom at the White House, saying she would rather sleep on the floor.

Harry Truman himself defended William Quantrill's actions and even attended two or three of the reunions of the former guerrilla's band that were held regularly in Independence. But if Truman is going back too far, if Henning writing in the 1960s is ancient history to you, then consider joining the many Kansas Citians who will go up to Kearney, Missouri, this year to enjoy the annual Jesse James Festival there.

Take in the rodeo or shooting competition, watch the demolition derby or cowboy fast-draw demonstration, but be careful not to bad talk the town's native son, who kept fighting twenty years after some folks said the war (according to Granny Clampett) "where the North tried to secede" was over.

A final note: near the Henning family grave plot in Independence Woodlawn Cemetery is a large monument for their neighbors, the Clampett family.

Don't Shout "Fire!"

In 1909 Kansas City, shouting "Fire!" in a crowded movie theater was probably a good idea. Fire Marshal Edward Trickett inspected forty theaters that year and had to caution the management of thirty-two of them about fire hazards in their buildings. Even after pushing for voluntary compliance, the chief ended up closing the National Theatre at 1112 Grand Avenue. The chief found abundant rubbish and paper still under the stage and throughout the auditorium after numerous promises by management to clean it up, and the room where the theater kept its motion picture machine was found to have defective wiring.

The chief said of the theaters, "Of the fifty running in this city, one-third are unsafe." On May 23, at the Majestic Theater on Walnut, film caught fire in the operator's

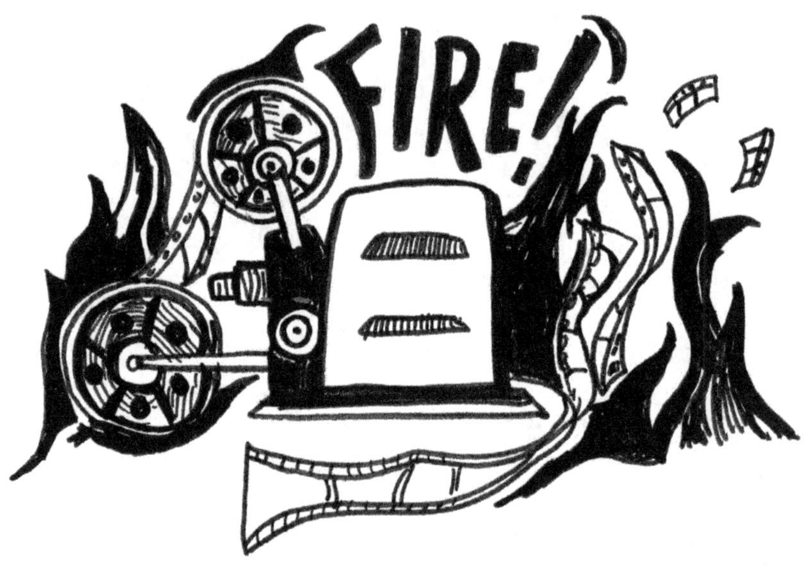

booth. A house singer took the stage and calmly quieted and led the crowd in song, keeping them occupied until the fire department arrived. On November 13, at the Cozy Theater at 1300 Main, the motion picture machine exploded and caught fire. The operator, Frank Tierney, had burns on his face and hands from trying to extinguish the fire.

Again, another explosion and fire came from the operator's booth in January 1910 at the Star nickel show on St. James Street in Kansas City, Kansas. Cries of "Fire!" were followed by a mad stampede for the rear exits. People trampled one another, and a large gate was literally torn from its hinges as the frightened crowd forced its way out. The theaters and wiring were bad enough, but what was not commonly understood in those early days was that the films themselves were explosive.

Film was made of nitrocellulose, which had a melting point a little over three hundred degrees Fahrenheit, while the film projector bulbs could reach an internal temperature of around five hundred degrees. A break in the film or a jam was all that was necessary to put the two in contact, and if the projectionist didn't quickly separate film from machine, the film would melt, catch fire and then explode. The fire that resulted was an additional problem; nitrocellulose film, once ignited, releases toxic gases and is extremely hard to extinguish. It will continue to burn under water.

In 1910, Eastman-Kodak came out with the first of many attempts at making a "safety" film, which was more flexible and less flammable. But it would be the 1950s before the film was used and the job of projectionist would be reasonably safe.

Star Movie

In 1917, the *Kansas City Star* hosted an event that would be unrivaled in the city's history. It would bring over forty-two thousand people through the doors of one building in a single day. In a room meant to hold twelve thousand people, sixteen thousand would pile in, as many as three to a seat, for the event of the season.

This wasn't an athletic contest, a political convention, a concert or a dance. No black ties or tuxedos were required, and no age limit was invoked, as alcohol was not part of the festivities. The record-breaking crowd was primarily made up of youngsters who came to see the new film *Snow White*. (This was long before Walt Disney made his version.)

The *Kansas City Star* had sponsored events in the past, but the turnout and response for this was unparalleled. Children outnumbered adults three to one and piled into every possible seat, aisle and doorway. One reported five children stacked up in two seats.

The first showing brought in over 14,000 attendees and the second over 16,000, with a final show, limited to adults, bringing in a paltry 11,000. In a town with a population of around 300,000, a children's movie sold 42,000 tickets in a single day, in a single theater. Nearly one hundred years later, the current record for largest attendance at a film screening is 27,022, set in Brazil at a football stadium in 2010.

He Lost Money on a Beatles Concert in the '60s?

The much-maligned Charles O. Finley, owner of the Kansas City Athletics and a Chicago insurance company owner, fired twelve managers in the seven years he was in town and constantly threatened to move the team, which he later did in 1967.

Finley had tried one publicity stunt after another to increase attendance at his faltering team's games. Some of the stunts included paying team members extra to grow moustaches, grazing sheep in the outfield during games and replacing the team mascot with a mule he named Charlie-O, which he brought to cocktail parties and into the pressroom. Finley used a robotic rabbit to deliver baseballs to the umpire; changed the team colors to gold, white and Kelly green; and would have the team ride into the stadium on mules. Kansas City fans, who wanted more substance and less show, almost universally disliked Finley.

Local media, especially the *Star*, felt they were being used by Finley and did as little as possible to promote the team. It was under these strained and unfortunate circumstances that Finley pulled off what he thought would be an incredible coup.

An up-and-coming sensational rock band that was doing its first U.S. tour had agreed to add an unscheduled concert at Municipal Stadium to its itinerary for the unheard-of sum of $150,000. At that time, it was the highest price ever paid for a single performance of a band. Finley had guaranteed the money regardless of ticket sales and had tied in the event with a charitable fundraiser for Children's Mercy Hospital (which he also guaranteed $25,000 regardless of ticket sales).

The stadium held thirty-five thousand, and the group, the Beatles, had been filling concert venues all across the country. Astonishingly, only twenty thousand fans showed up for the thirty-one-minute, twelve-song concert. Finley had a picture of himself wearing a Beatles wig printed on the back of every ticket. Finley lost nearly $40,000 in 1964 bringing the Beatles to Kansas City, and they never played here again.

There were some good things to come from the concert: Children's Mercy got a nice donation and twenty thousand lucky fans got to hear some of the Beatles' hit songs, including an old song from the playlist from their days touring with Little Richard: "Kansas City/Hey, Hey, Hey." The song was fresh in the musicians' minds a month later when they were recording their next album and didn't have enough original songs ready to record. They chose to do a cover of the song and recorded it in one take. The album sold over 800,000 copies in 1965 alone, and the single was released on the flip side of *Boys*, selling hundreds of thousands more copies.

Finley took the Athletics to Oakland in 1967. The Beatles never performed in Kansas City again; however,

Paul McCartney did return in 1993 during his New World Tour and, for the only performance of the tour, brought back an old song he'd sung here almost thirty years before: "Kansas City/Hey, Hey, Hey."

BOONE TOWN

When people think of Daniel Boone, the buckskin-clad Kentuckian in a coonskin cap is the first image that comes to mind. While Boone did live in Kentucky, Pennsylvania and Tennessee, his explorations went far beyond those states, and he spent many of his later years in Missouri. Daniel Boone traveled through this area in 1816 on a hunting trip with a hunter named Indian Phillips, stopping at Fort Osage on the way west and staying at Fort Leavenworth in 1817 on the way back. He saw parts of Kansas and Nebraska and may have pushed up into the Dakota Territory as well.

Boone had been preceded in exploration here by his sons, Daniel Morgan Boone (the first American known to have come to the Kansas City area) and Nathan (who led Captain William Clark overland to establish Fort Osage near the Missouri River, east of Kansas City, in 1808).

Daniel Boone would visit the fort in 1816 and go exploring into Indian Territory from there. Eighty-two-year-old Daniel Boone came back through the area in

1817 and ended up in Fort Leavenworth at some point on the return trip. He returned to his home in Defiance, Missouri, where he died in 1820. But his children and grandchildren would help populate the area: Daniel Morgan Boone had twelve children, his sister Susannah Boone-Hayes had ten and Nathan Boone fathered fourteen. Many of their descendants would live in Kansas City and other parts of Missouri.

Daniel Morgan Boone was the third son of Daniel Boone. He arrived near the mouth of the Kaw as early as 1786 and ran traps along the Blue River and Brush Creek. He served as a captain in the War of 1812 and then returned to trapping. He later moved into Kansas Territory to work several years as a government farmer to the Indians. In 1831, Daniel Morgan and his family moved to Westport Township. Boone settled down to farm and bought land near Sixty-third and Woodland, where he lived until his death in 1839. Some of his land would eventually become part of the original Blue Hills Golf Course. In 1837, he sold part of his land to his nephew, Daniel Boone Hays (son of his sister Susannah Boone and her husband, William Hays). Two years later, a cholera epidemic hit Kansas City, taking many lives, including that of Daniel Morgan Boone. He was buried on his farm, and the grave is in the Boone-Hays Cemetery at Sixty-third and Euclid in the Daniel Morgan Boone Park.

Van Daniel Boone, son of Jesse and grandson of Daniel Boone, was married in Independence, Missouri, in 1845.

His sister Panthea Grant Boone also lived in Independence for a while with her husband, Missouri governor Lilburn Boggs. Another brother, Albert Gallatin Boone, owned a tavern in Westport that became a gathering place for proslavery forces during the border war. His tavern/trading post at 500 Westport Road is still a popular gathering place (Kelly's Westport Inn) and is the oldest remaining building in Kansas City.

One of the great-grandchildren of Daniel Boone was Confederate colonel Upton Hays, who was in the Battle of Carthage, had to take over command in the First Battle of Independence and led at the Battles of Lone Jack and First Newtonia (where he died in battle).

Daniel Boone's many descendants have continued to make their mark on Missouri history, and many live in and around the Kansas City area. In fact, in 2010, the Boone Society Inc. (which includes descendants, genealogists and historians) had its biennial family reunion in Kansas City, and members went to see the Boone sites associated with the famous explorer's many descendants who helped settle Kansas City.

BRIDGE TO THE FUTURE

The history of Kansas City is like that of any town—a mix of triumph and tragedy. On July 3, 1869, it was triumph that ruled. Years of effort, advocating, politicking and investment by city visionaries was finally paying off. A rail line connected the city to Chicago and points east, and the first railroad bridge (Hannibal and St. Joseph) across the Missouri River was officially opened. The hero of the day was Chicago and Alton engineer Octave Chanute, who had spent the previous two years directing the building of the bridge.

Chanute was educated in Paris, and his father was a professor d'art in France. When Chanute came to town, there was only one small foundry. He had to fashion tools, build derricks and dredges, build parts and teach new methods to workers, as well as design the bridge. Spanning a river that flooded regularly and had risen as much as forty-eight feet in the past was no small task. The first footings Chanute tried were toppled by the force of the current. He fixed that problem by using a new type of footing that had been used in Germany to bridge the Rhine. In order to put the footings in place, Chanute sent men under water in diving suits supplied with air-through hoses. He also designed a submersible room for them to work in. When the bridge was finally completed, festivities were in order, and one of the biggest celebrations the city had ever known ensued.

As many as forty thousand people were believed to have attended the event. There were brass bands, governors from seven states and dignitaries from dozens of towns who joined the locals in celebration. At Twelfth and

Troost, a spread of barbecued turkey, beef and chicken paid for by the city was laid out on tables one hundred feet long, sufficient to feed everyone who came. A balloon aeronaut ascended into the sky, and fireworks followed. A lavish banquet was given by Kearsey Coates at a hotel at Fifth and Broadway for dignitaries, social leaders and investors. A ten-foot-long cake that was made to look like the bridge was served, and a dress ball and fireworks finished out the evening.

In the next fifteen years, seven more railroads would come to town, and Kansas City would become a major rail hub and a great shipping center for Midwest grain and beef. The Kansas City Stockyards, built in 1871, were also designed by Chanute. A rail station larger than any in the world outside of New York City's Central and Pennsylvania Stations was built. The stockyards in Kansas City were the second largest in the nation. Armour, Swift and others would build processing plants in the river bottoms, producing thousands of jobs, and the city would grow from a measly 3,500 people in 1865 to 32,000 in 1870 and to 132,000 by 1890. By the 1940s, Union Station would be handling two hundred passenger trains a day for the town of 400,000.

The grand designer who made it all happen, Octave Chanute, continued to design bridges, including one at Sibley, Missouri, just east of Kansas City. Chanute established the first commercial plants for pressure-treated railroad ties that would last longer and conserve wood.

And in order to keep track of the age of timbers used on bridges and under rails, he introduced the use of the dated railroad spike in the United States. During the building of the Hannibal Bridge, Octave Chanute would relax by flying kites over the bluffs overlooking the river while he watched his work progress. This hobby led Chanute into a whole new field after his career with the railroads.

By the 1890s, Chanute had moved on to designing multi-wing gliders. Using his talent as a structural engineer, he designed some of the strongest and lightest gliders of his time and would become a pioneer in aviation design. He corresponded with the Wright brothers, exchanging hundreds of letters between 1900 and 1910, aiding and encouraging their efforts. Wilbur Wright gave the eulogy at Chanute's funeral in 1910. His many accomplishments could fairly include making it possible for a small town to become a cow town and a cow town to become a city.

Look at the Ears on that Clown

A number of movie actors came from or lived in the Kansas City area at some point in their lives. When Bill (Clark) Gable turned twenty-one, he inherited $300 from his grandfather and, against his father's wishes, set out to find his fortune as an actor.

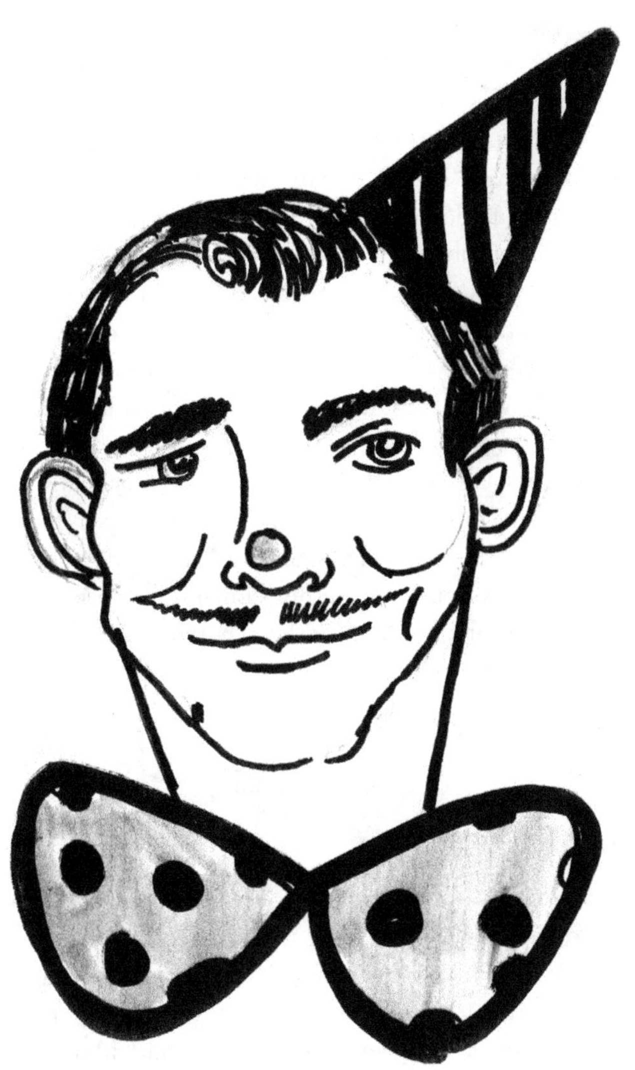

Billy Gable moved to Kansas City and joined a troupe of actors called the Jewel Players in 1922. At that time, a lot of traveling shows started their tours in Kansas City. While in town, Gable helped the troupe by putting up tents, playing in the orchestra (French horn) and selling tickets. Gable particularly hated one method the troupe used to drum up a crowd for its shows. He said it "was the most God-awful thing." He would have to dress up in a clown suit and join the band on the street corner, playing "Marching Through Georgia" over and over again. The Jewel Players wound up broke in Oregon, and Gable had to work in a lumber mill just to survive.

Both Clark Gable and Walt Disney were learning how hard you had to work to make it in show business in Kansas City at the same time. The year 1922 might have been a hard year for them, but whether clowning around on the street corners or playing Charlie Chaplin, their roads to Hollywood started here.

Promised Land

Once upon a time, twenty thousand homeless people came to Kansas City. Many, if not most, were hungry and broke, refugees from a place where they had no protection from their enemies, no sympathy and no redress in the law. Their government had abandoned them to local thugs and left them with little hope. Attempts at reconstructing the Old South were abandoned in 1877, leaving the black populace to the mercy of former Rebels, Klansmen and a white culture that could not accept them as equals.

Violence against blacks rose; intimidation and murder closed off opportunities for advancement to the generation that had lived to see emancipation and the hope it offered. Leaders, including former slaves Benjamin "Pap" Singleton and Henry Adams, came forward preaching a new hope, a promised land in the West. Though there was no promise made, there was at least hope in the land where John Brown and the abolitionists had stopped slavery's advance. They came by the thousands, often spending all they had just to get here, risking all they had just to leave.

There wasn't room for them all, so they made their own room, building shantytowns just over the Kansas line in Wyandotte. New communities like Juniper Town (on the bluffs near the Kawsmouth) and Rattlebone Hollow (near Jersey Creek) seemed to appear overnight. Boatloads came, even in winter, and found themselves stranded, cold and hungry, in Kansas City. Relief organizations tried to help, but there wasn't enough to go around. The migrants just had to help themselves. Many found work in town, but most would move on farther into Kansas, Oklahoma or Colorado. False rumors of free land in Kansas had driven some of the groups here, while others were organized and ready to purchase land and start fresh. Pap Singleton led group after group out of the South. They sang, "Marching along, yes, we are marching along—to Kansas City we are bound. We have Mister Singleton for our president; he will go on before us and lead us through. Marching along, we are marching along to reach K.C. at the gate of our promised land."

They were met with a mixed reaction. This was Jayhawker country, a place where the fight against slavery had been tooth and nail. There were some who had fought that fight and welcomed the weary travelers, but they also were met with fear and prejudice. What would be done with so many poor people? In 1879, Sojourner Truth called it the "greatest movement of all time" and came to help. Clara Brown brought donations from Colorado and came to help.

During the ten years that followed the initial wave of exodusters, twenty thousand acres of Kansas land was purchased, thirty-three towns were begun, many homesteads cropped up and thousands of southern blacks made Kansas their new home. In 1860, the black population of Kansas was 625 free men and two slaves; by 1870, it was 17,000, and by 1880, it was 60,000. Many of Kansas City's families can trace their presence here to the great exodus of the 1870s and the trek to the "promised land" in Kansas.

Shoe Parties and Biscuits

In 1882, Jacob Loose quit his dry goods business in Chetopa, Kansas, purchased the Corle Cracker and Candy Company and set up shop in Kansas City. The company would change names a few times: to Loose Brothers Manufacturing in 1885 and the American Biscuit Company in 1895. In 1902, brothers Jacob and Joseph Loose partnered with Joseph Wiles to form the Loose-Wiles Biscuit Company. Loose was a member of the board of the National Biscuit Company (Nabisco) in 1902, but he liquidated his holdings to start Loose-Wiles.

Nabisco would end up being Loose-Wiles's largest competitor. Believing sunshine was healthful for workers, the Loose-Wiles plant was built with many windows, and they named the crackers and cookies produced there "Sunshine Biscuits." The name caught on, and the product line was extremely successful. Jacob Loose became a rich and influential man, and he and his wife, Ella, were able to live a comfortable lifestyle and contribute greatly to the improvement of conditions in their town. For thirty years, Mrs. Loose sponsored annual Thanksgiving "shoe parties" for children from the Gillis Orphan home. Each child at the party would receive a dollar and a new pair of shoes. Jacob Loose passed away in 1923, and Ella used some of the fortune they had amassed from the cracker business to build a fitting memorial to him.

Loose Park was the result. Loose Park is now one of Kansas City's most popular parks; the land had been, at various times, part of an old homestead, a Civil War battleground and a golf course. Mrs. Loose purchased the land from the Hugh Ward estate and gave it to the city in 1927. Loose Park is home to Kansas City's municipal rose garden, covering one and a half acres and containing about four thousand roses of 150 varieties. It has walking trails, a lake, a playground, a spray ground, tennis courts, picnic areas, a rain garden and an arboretum. Civil War markers and cannons mark the command of Major General Sterling Price and Confederate gun placements during the Battle of Westport. In 1941, Mrs. Loose presented the park with a statue of her husband, which was placed at the main entrance at Fifty-first Street and Wornall Road. In addition to the Looses' other charities, upon Jacob's death in 1923, the Jacob Loose Million-Dollar Charity Fund Association was established. It was Kansas City's first million-dollar foundation. In 1989, the Jacob L. and Ella C. Loose Foundation fund was started at the Greater Kansas City Community Foundation and Affiliated Trusts, and it continues to serve the citizens of Kansas City.

The business Jacob Loose had built continued to grow long after he was gone. In 1946, Sunshine Biscuits, Inc., had several plants, including the Thousand Window Bakery in New York, which at that time was the largest bakery in the world. A new plant was built in the Fairfax district in Kansas City in 1949, with a 550-foot continuous oven that is currently the largest in the world. In 1996, Sunshine merged with the Keebler Company. The Fairfax plant continues to produce popular brands like Cheez-Its, Krispy Crackers and (sometimes) Hydrox cookies, and the company Jacob Loose started still makes millions of crackers (not to mention, millions of dollars) while continuing to employ Kansas City workers.

BARBECUE KINGS

According to the 1911 *Kansas City Star*, he was "crowned" fifteen years earlier in Kentucky by Senator Breckinridge or some other such dignitary who was between drinks at a picnic. Henry Perry, the "Barbecue King," spoke about his experience and the technique that set him apart as a purveyor of what would become Kansas City's most famous food. Though slow cooking meat goes back long before there was a town at the mouth of the Kaw, it was the barbecue kings of the early twentieth century, like Henry Perry, who developed the slow-roasted, rubbed and seasoned meats that make Kansas City the barbecue capital of the world.

Perry started his business in 1908, working from a stand at Banks Street Alley, near the garment district. He soon moved to a roomier location at Seventeenth and Lydia. He had learned his technique back in Memphis while working as a cook on a steamboat, but he perfected it once he came to Kansas City and became his own boss. By 1911, he was advertising in the *Kansas City Sun*: "During the Holidays Call on Perry for your Barbecued Meats, O'Possum, Ground Hog, Coon, Beef, Pork and Mutton. Wholesale and Retail the Best in the City. Henry Perry the Barbecue King 1514 E. 19th St."

That's right, Perry cooked a larger variety of animals than you normally see in a modern barbecue joint. He said a barbecue king "has to be able to barbecue any kind of meat better than anybody else." Perry slow cooked meat over a brick-lined pit that was three feet wide by three feet deep by ten feet long. He'd have the fire going for a day before the meat went on the grill and would often cook meats for twenty-four hours. Perry said, "I've never seen the meat yet I couldn't barbecue. That goes for sheep, hogs, geese, chicken, fish, rabbits, squirrels, 'possums, oysters, and most everything you ever heard of. And this barbecue system is getting more popular with the white folks too."

He was right. Although the sauce he used was strong and peppery, the tender meats he sold were popular with workers in the garment district where he started and with everyone in the Nineteenth and Vine area where his stand had moved by 1911. Perry moved his business from a tent to an old streetcar. The *Star* reported in 1919 that the Barbecue King had abandoned the old "palace" (streetcar) for "more pretentious quarters": a streetcar barn. Perry believed he was blessed in his success, and he gave back generously. In 1920, he served a free barbecue dinner to one thousand "old men, women and children" in a vacant lot behind his restaurant. One of Henry's employees, Charles Bryant, inherited his business when he passed away in 1940 and then sold it to his brother, Arthur (who had also worked for Perry), in 1946.

Arthur Bryant would take Henry's sauce, add a tomato base and balance the hot pepper taste with more molasses for a sweet and tangy sauce that became the favorite of locals and visitors from all over the country. Bryant would spend the rest of his life at the top of the barbecue game. He was sometimes called "King Arthur," but he wasn't the only claimant to the throne. Another employee of Perry's, Arthur Pinkard, would join forces with Ollie Gates in 1946 at a storefront location near Nineteenth and Vine to create another Kansas City barbecue dynasty. Originally advertised as Kentucky Bar-B-Q, and later as Gates Bar-B-Q, Gates's sauce does not contain molasses and comes in styles from sweet and mild to extra hot. There are a half dozen popular Gates restaurants in Kansas City, and the sauces and rubs can be purchased in grocery stores and online.

Today, Kansas City can confidently claim to be the barbecue capital of the world, with more barbecue restaurants per capita than any other city in the world and two of the biggest barbecue competitions in the nation: the Great Lenexa Barbecue Battle and the American

Royal Barbecue. It is home to the Kansas City Barbecue Society (the world's largest organization of barbecue enthusiasts, with fifteen thousand members worldwide), which acts as the sanctioning body of over four hundred barbecue competitions. Just think, all this from the humble beginnings of a little tent where you could get a tasty Christmas opossum.

KANSAS CITY DRAG QUEENS

There's nothing new under the sun, just look in the old *Stars*. In the November 26, 1880 issue of the *Kansas City Evening Star*, the reader is introduced to the "queer world" of female impersonators, explaining their "manners, customs, life and amusements." The article starts with interviews of stage performers—"A queer set of men who make thirty to one hundred and fifty dollars per week by aping the frailer and fairer sex"—and then goes on to discuss the cross-dressing lifestyle. Stating, "There are worlds within worlds, circles within circles," the *Star* delves into the foibles and misunderstandings that arose from male theatergoers becoming enamored with what they thought were female performers. The performers would laugh and discuss the lavish gifts and attention poured on them by unsuspecting men. They claimed dozens of admirers in Kansas City had been "smitten with their bogus charms."

The two female impersonators (whose stage names were Lansing and St. Leon) the *Star* interviewed would shed their costume and personas when they left the theater. However, they explained that some other actors in their line kept the "act" going all the time, going out in public dressed as women. In Chicago, the reporter explains, there is a large community of such men, and *even* in Kansas City they can be found. One performer, Gus Mills, was said to live entirely as a woman, to the point of sewing his own costumes and falling in love with other men.

The *Star* said of Gus: "As a female impersonator he draws a large salary and is a most remarkable success, but as a man he is a gigantic failure and not worth the powder that would blow his effeminated soul to purgatory." Finally, the article discusses the culture of female impersonators and the "drag" parties they would have, which had to be kept quiet, as "the police would not hesitate to raid them."

The report ends with an air of mystery and amusement, as if it were perfectly acceptable for the *Star* to give the reader a free peek into the tent at a sideshow but inappropriate for him to go and buy a ticket. In objective reporting circa 1880, the *Star* writer pandered to Victorian values while titillating readers with a taboo subject. The reporter didn't rate a byline, but one has to wonder if he might have been an ancestor of Jerry Springer?

Monarchs of Baseball, Too

In 1908, baseball was segregated in Kansas City, and everywhere else for that matter. The spring season greeted a new Negro team called the Monarchs, formerly the J.W. Jenkinses after the sponsor, J.W. Jenkins of Jenkins Music Company. The Monarchs were a popular team, and in 1920 a new infusion of talent was added to their roster when J.L. Wilkinson of Des Moines, Iowa, took over and brought in players from the All-Nations and an Arizona army team. Wilkinson knew his team had talent and a following; he convinced the Kansas City Blues of the American Association League to play a post-season series against the Monarchs in 1921. The Blues won that year, five games to three, but it wasn't a walkover, and the local fans came out in large numbers to support both teams. The next year, the Blues finished the season in third place and once again played a post-season series against the Monarchs. Interracial games in those days presented a challenge to the social order. Many did not like the idea of whites even competing against blacks, and there was a fear that losing to the "inferior" race would upset societal norms. In 1922, the Monarchs upset the norm, winning five out of six games against the highly rated Blues. The result sent a ripple through the American League, and Commissioner Thomas J. Hickey banned interleague (thus interracial) play for all American League teams.

The year 1921 had seen Babe Ruth and his All-Stars lose a showdown with baseball commissioner Judge Kennesaw Mountain Landis. The team, which included players who were in that year's World Series, had barnstormed the country after regular season play, a practice that had incurred only minor fines from the league in previous years. Landis threatened Ruth. Ruth ignored the threat, and Landis suspended Ruth from play and fined him a whopping $3,300 (his share of income from the World Series). Ruth canceled the tour but was suspended from the first five weeks of the 1922 season. Fans, including President Harding, cried foul. Landis backed away from the fine, and after seeing the loss in revenue from the games Ruth missed, the owners dropped the rule. Ruth immediately set up another tour. As before, he scheduled games against Negro League teams. Ruth liked the competition and turnout for interracial games. His willingness to play against and associate with black players was unusual for his day, and in some parts of the country, it put him and his team at risk of violence from the Klan.

On October 22, 1922, Babe Ruth went four for four, but his team of All-Stars still lost to the Kansas City Monarchs. The Monarchs of 1922 had proven they were every bit as good a team as any in the white leagues. Still, beating a team with World Series talent and the best hitter in the game wasn't enough for the owners and the commissioner of baseball. Although Landis was not solely responsible for keeping baseball segregated, in his twenty-plus years as commissioner, he did nothing to advance integration, nor did the majority of team owners. The Kansas City Monarchs provided a home and proving ground for some of baseball's greatest players during the reign of Judge Landis as commissioner. The team won the first Negro League World Series in 1924 and had only one losing season in its entire franchise history.

Former Monarchs led the way when integration began in 1946. A Monarch in 1945 and a Royal in 1946, Jackie Robinson broke the major-league color line when he was brought up from the Montreal Royals to play for the Brooklyn Dodgers in 1947. The next year, forty-two-year-old former Monarch Satchel Paige would be signed by the Cleveland Indians. A trickle became a flood. With integration, the Negro League began to fade away, as both minor-league and major-league baseball cherry picked the ranks of its best players.

The Kansas City Monarchs sent more players to the Major Leagues than any other Negro League team in history. After fifty-seven years of providing a home for some of baseball's true unrecognized royalty, the Monarchs finally disbanded in 1965.

From Orphan to Congressman

Henry Lee Jost came to Missouri from the Five Points Mission for Homeless Children in New York City in 1873. He was one of over ten thousand children who would be placed in Missouri and Kansas by the Children's Aid Society between 1854 and 1929. The organization was founded by Charles Loring Brace in 1853. Agents for the charity were tasked with finding suitable homes in small towns and on farms for children who were orphaned, runaways, unwanted or just came from large impoverished families and wanted to get a better life.

The "orphans" were brought west by train, and agents would advertise in small towns and communities the availability of children and the need for homes. Rather than a massive wave, the children were brought out in groups of fewer than one hundred at a time. Jost was part of a group of twenty. According to Mr. E. Trott, who was taking a group of twenty-three children ages four to fourteen to Lawrence on January 6, 1882, he had made 143 such trips and was one of three agents taking a group west every two weeks.

In 1887, an agent for the organization stated, "We send three to five thousand children out of New York City every year." The cost at that time for transportation was twenty dollars per child. Groups came through Union Station regularly, and many of the "farm" communities they were placed in are now suburbs, or soon to be so, of Greater Kansas City. Groups of children were brought to Paola, Belton, Louisburg, Ottawa, Osawatomie, Bucyrus, Eudora and Lawrence, as well as to Kansas City. Prospective parents from outlying communities would sometimes come to Union Station to review and "get first pick" of the children. One group being taken to Belton in 1897 included a five-year-old boy who said he was one of seven children whose father had died and whose mother had been forced into the poorhouse. He was optimistic, though, saying, "I am going to a nice home now."

Seven-year-old Henry Lee Jost was transported to a little town in northwestern Missouri, but he spent most of his adult life in Kansas City. He went to the Kansas City Law School. He served as an assistant prosecutor for the city and took part in examining witnesses in the infamous Swope Trial. He was elected mayor of Kansas City, Missouri, in 1912, serving during the construction of Union Station and the establishment of the Federal Reserve Bank. He was called the "orphan boy" mayor, and his rise from poverty was used to gain sympathy and votes. In 1922, Jost was elected to the United States Congress. He served one term and then returned to his successful law practice in Kansas City.

Henry Jost was but one of thousands of orphans plucked from the streets of New York who grew and thrived in the Midwest. According to Children's Aid Society records, many of its "boys" made good, including a governor of a state, a governor of a territory, two congressmen, four members of state legislatures, eight postmasters, two sheriffs, twenty-seven bankers, twenty-one clergymen and various others in prominent positions. Some 150,000 children were placed by the society, and it is estimated that they may have as many as 2 million descendants.

Whoppers

The size of Missouri catfish is both a source of pride and a starting point for exaggeration. The current "official" world record is a 130-pound, 57-inch-long blue catfish caught in the Missouri River in 2010. The next largest variety of catfish is the flathead. Again, the state record fish was a 99-pounder also caught from the Missouri River. From the earliest records in Kansas City, the catfish was an important source of food and a popular target for anglers.

In the territorial Kansas days, there was the Catfish Hotel at the southeast corner of State Avenue and Fourth Street. It was a four-room log building run by Isaac Brown (a Wyandotte Indian). Men working for the surveyor general stayed there when the border was being surveyed, and at that time it was just known as Brown's. That year, the spring thaw caused an ice floe that shoved a large number of catfish out onto the banks at the Kawspoint, stranding them. The easy pickings were gathered and prepared by

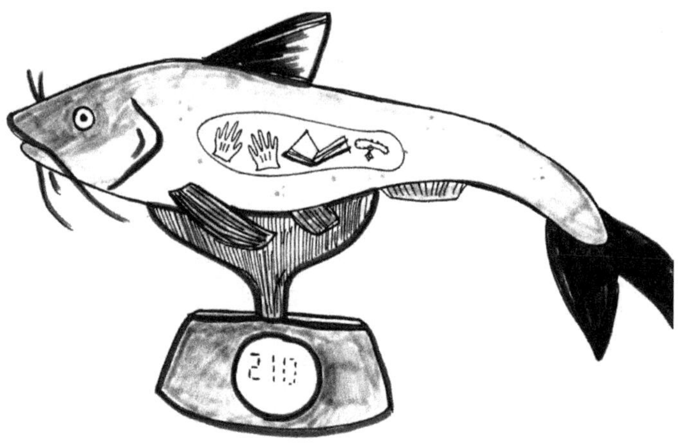

Thomas J. Barker, the resident cook. The workmen liked the fare so well that they rechristened Brown's the Catfish Hotel, where the dish became a regular item on the menu.

The *Kansas City Star* reported catfish stories, true and exaggerated equally, throughout the long history of this area. In 1882, the *Star* reported that a wrecked ship was found by the presence of a large catfish nearby that was dead drunk on the whiskey from its hold. In 1886, the *Star* explained how catfish dealt with the river being low by shaving off their whiskers and living ashore with the other Missourians. In 1887, the *Star* reported that the largest fish ever taken out of the Missouri was a six-foot, four-inch catfish that weighed 210 pounds caught in 1885. In 1889, it lamented that catfish were eating up the wheat crop in parts of Kansas (a wet year). By 1889, a fishing party reported catching a 280-pounder.

In 1914, old settlers' tales included a story of a catfish that trapped itself in a calf lot during an overflow of the river and was found to have swallowed a bear! One story even told about a six-foot, nine-inch, 210-pound catfish that had a gold bracelet, a settler dog, a pair of buckskin gloves and seven copies of the city ordinances found in its belly. Kansas Citians continue to enjoy catching and eating the whiskered river whale. Visitors can hire professional fishing guide Captain Catfish or fill up at one of the chain of local restaurants called Jumpin' Catfish. At the time of this writing, you could also go to the Bass Pro in Independence, Missouri, and see the 100-plus-pound catfish named Bess (after Bess Truman). Bess was caught in the Missouri River and now is the boss of the aquarium there. Seriously, she ate a 7-pound bass that was put in to be on display with her. They have to lock up the fudge shop at night to keep her out. We put a saddle on her and let my grandkids ride her around the aquarium. OK, but the first one was true.

FROG RANCH

The communities surrounding Kansas City have always found a ready market in the larger town for their produce and livestock. The City Market and various smaller farmers' markets thrive on products brought in from the nearby rural communities. South of Kansas City is the town of LaCygne, Kansas, situated near the Marais des Cygnes River. There is an abundance of water and marshes in the area. For many years, Linn County was the bullfrog belt, producing frogs so large and plentiful that they were a source of legend. Locals bragged of catching frogs there the size of jackrabbits, weighing up to ten pounds apiece. The large number of bullfrogs that resided near LaCygne was a popular source of food and easy income for locals, who would sell them at the markets in Kansas City.

In 1909, dealers were paying $2.00 to $3.50 a dozen for frog legs in Kansas City. That same year, a plan to start a froggery was instituted in LaCygne. The previous year's crop had been disappointing, and the easy pickings of an afternoon of five dozen frogs suddenly seemed to be a thing of the past.

Accordingly, the LaCygne Frog Propagating and Export Company was formed and reported to the *Kansas City Star*. The company proposed to lease Ox Bow Lake and stock it with healthy bullfrogs. The group, made up of local citizens, planned on raising frogs that would be guaranteed under the pure food laws. They were to have a frog hospital and experimenting station under the supervision of Dr. Wells and Dr. Brentlinger.

The physicians planned to breed a frog that was all legs and croakless. The muscle wasted developing the chest and lungs for croaking would be eliminated, and the legs would be the beneficiaries. The doctors were to examine all the frogs, and any that looked likely to catch pneumonia from wet feet were to be removed from the herd. The rest were to be fed on milk and honey so as to impart a better flavor.

Though the men from LaCygne had a little fun pulling the leg of the *Star* reporter over their enterprise, a number of serious froggers did jump into the business in the early 1900s.

Kansas State Fisheries warden Del W. Travis even started raising the critters at the state fish hatchery to study the potential for profit for Kansas farmers. Travis said, "The demand for frog legs is enormous; fabulous prices are being paid by hotels, restaurants and private families for this much desired table delicacy." In fact, business was really "hopping" for a dealer in Michigan, who shipped 17,350 dozen frog legs to restaurants across the country in a single season.

Not all the frogs in LaCygne ended up "croaking," and the population eventually recovered. But the LaCygne Frog Propagating and Export Company never quite made the big splash it was hoping for.

Bibliography

Books

Bell, J. Boyer. *Cheating and Deception.* New York: St. Martin's Press, 1982.

Bullard, Loring. *Healing Waters: Missouri's Historic Mineral Springs and Spas.* Columbia: University of Missouri Press, 2004.

Burnes, Brian, Robert W. Butler and Dan Viets. *Walt Disney's Missouri.* Kansas City, MO: Kansas City Star Books, 2002.

Christensen, Lawrence O. *Dictionary of Missouri Biography.* Columbia: University of Missouri Press, 1999.

Clifford, Amber R. "Prostitution and Reform in Kansas City, 1880–1930." In *The Other Missouri History: Populists, Prostitutes and Regular Folk*. Edited by Thomas M. Spencer. Columbia, MO: University of Missouri Press, 2004.

Cook, Kevin. *Titanic Thompson: The Man Who Bet on Everything.* New York: W.W. Norton and Co., 2010.

Curtis, William J. *The Truman Neighborhood: From Elegant Mansions to the Neck.* Independence, MO: Arrow Printing, 2004.

Dalton, Reverend William J. *The Life of Father Bernard Donnelley*. Kansas City: Grimes-Joyce Printing Co., 1921.

DeAngelo, Dory. *Voices Across Time*. Kansas City, MO: Tapestry Publications, 1987.

———. *What About Kansas City*. Kansas City, MO: Two Lane Press, 1995.

DeVol, George H. *Forty Years a Gambler on the Mississippi.* Cincinnati, OH: Devol & Haines, 1887.

Dodd, Monroe. *Kansas City Crime Central*. Kansas City, MO: Kansas City Star Books, 2010.

Gillis, Delia C. *Kansas City* (MO). Black America Series. Charleston, SC: Arcadia, 2007.

Houdini, Harry. *The Adventurous Life of a Versatile Artist: Houdini.* New York, 1922.

James, Jesse, Jr., *Jesse James, My Father*. Cleveland, OH: Buckeye Publishing Co., 1899.

James, Laura. *The Love Pirate and the Bandit's Son: Murder, Sin and Scandal in the Shadow of Jesse James.* New York: Sterling Publishing Co., Inc, n.d.

Katz, William Loren. *The Black West.* 1971. Reprint, New York: Harlem Moon, Broadway Books, a division of Random House, Ethrac Publications, 2005.

Larkin, Lew. *Missouri Heritage.* Vol. 2. Point Lookout, MO: School of the Ozarks Press, 1971.

Larsen, Lawrence H., and Nancy Hulsten. *Pendergast.* Columbia: University of Missouri Press, 1997.

McCullough, David. *Truman.* New York: Simon & Schuster, 1992.

Morgan, Perl W. *History of Wyandotte County Kansas and its People.* Chicago: Lewis Publishing, 1911.

Morgan, Robert. *Boone: A Biography.* Chapel Hill, NC: Algonquin Books of Chapel Hill, 2007.

Paxton, Heather N. *The American Royal: 1899–1999.* Kansas City: American Royal Association BK MK Press, University of Missouri, 1999.

Priddy, Bob. *Across Our Wide Missouri.* Vol. 3, *More Stories.* Independence, MO: Independence Press Herald Publishing House, 1994.

Randolph, Vance. *Vance Randolph in the Ozarks.* Branson, MO: Ozarks Mountaineer, 1981.

Sandy, Wilda. *Here Lies Kansas City.* Kansas City, MO: Bennett Schneider Inc., 1984.

Simonson, John. *Paris of the Plains.* Charleston, SC: The History Press, 2010.

Spicer, Chrystopher J. *Clark Gable: Biography, Filmography, Bibliography.* Jefferson, NC: McFarland & Co., 2002.

Stillwell, Ted W. *Portraits of the Past.* Vol. 2. Independence, MO: The Examiner: Benjamin Weir Jr., Pub., 2002.

Vestal, Stanley. *The Missouri.* Lincoln, NE: University of Nebraska Press, 1996.

Wayne, Jane Ellen. *The Leading Men of M.G.M.* New York: Caroll & Graf Pub., 2004.

Wilcox, Pearl. *Independence and Twentieth Century Pioneer.* Independence, MO: Jackson County Historical Society, 1976.

Wood, Larry. *Ozark Gunfights and Other Notorious Incidents.* Gretna, LA: Pelican, 2010.

Young, Josh. *Missouri Curiosities.* Guilford, CT: Morris Book Publishers, 2010.

Young, William H., and Nathan B. Young. *Your Kansas City and Mine.* Kansas City, MO: Midwest Afro-American Genealogy Interest Coalition, 1950, 1997.

NEWSPAPERS

Dallas Morning News. "Untitled." February 24, 2008.

Independence [Missouri] *Examiner.* "Two Nuns Help Chase Down Robber." August 13, 2009.

Kansas City [Missouri] *Journal.* "Adam God to Drop Plea of Insanity." May 22, 1909.

———. "Again Hurt Going to Fire." December 16, 1909.

———. "The Barnum Show." October 3, 1884.

———. "Bullets Kill Two and Wound Five in Fierce Battle Between Police and Band of Religious Fanatics." December 9, 1908.

———. "Cozy Theater." November 19, 1909.

———. "Fire Warden Closes National Theater." October 14, 1909.

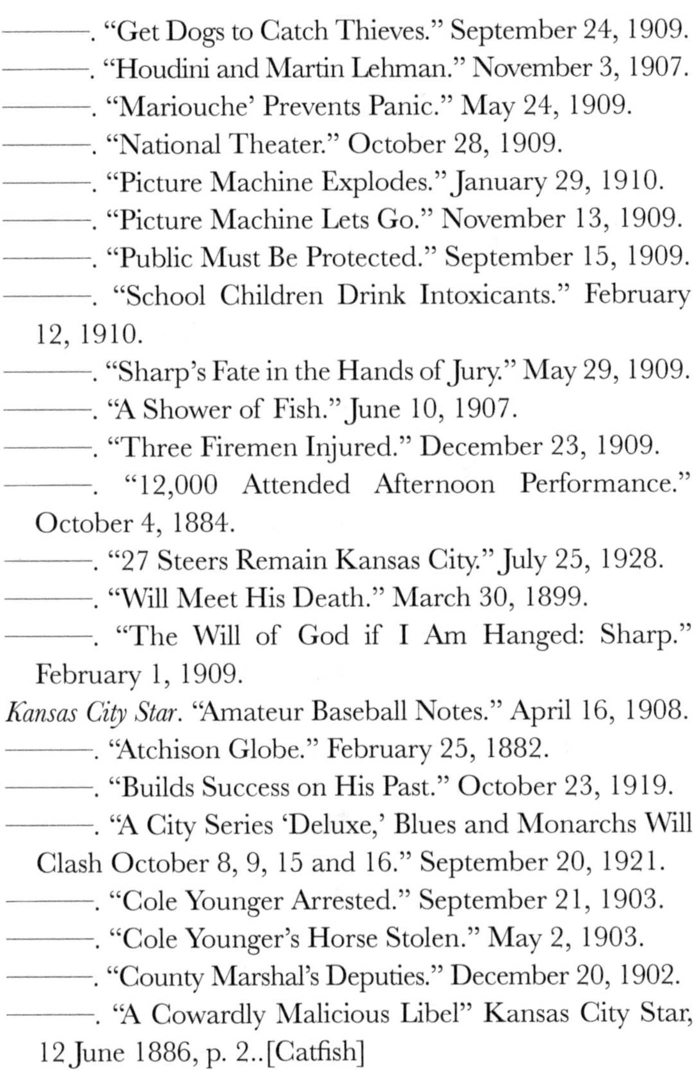

———. "Get Dogs to Catch Thieves." September 24, 1909.

———. "Houdini and Martin Lehman." November 3, 1907.

———. "Mariouche' Prevents Panic." May 24, 1909.

———. "National Theater." October 28, 1909.

———. "Picture Machine Explodes." January 29, 1910.

———. "Picture Machine Lets Go." November 13, 1909.

———. "Public Must Be Protected." September 15, 1909.

———. "School Children Drink Intoxicants." February 12, 1910.

———. "Sharp's Fate in the Hands of Jury." May 29, 1909.

———. "A Shower of Fish." June 10, 1907.

———. "Three Firemen Injured." December 23, 1909.

———. "12,000 Attended Afternoon Performance." October 4, 1884.

———. "27 Steers Remain Kansas City." July 25, 1928.

———. "Will Meet His Death." March 30, 1899.

———. "The Will of God if I Am Hanged: Sharp." February 1, 1909.

Kansas City Star. "Amateur Baseball Notes." April 16, 1908.

———. "Atchison Globe." February 25, 1882.

———. "Builds Success on His Past." October 23, 1919.

———. "A City Series 'Deluxe,' Blues and Monarchs Will Clash October 8, 9, 15 and 16." September 20, 1921.

———. "Cole Younger Arrested." September 21, 1903.

———. "Cole Younger's Horse Stolen." May 2, 1903.

———. "County Marshal's Deputies." December 20, 1902.

———. "A Cowardly Malicious Libel" Kansas City Star, 12 June 1886, p. 2..[Catfish]

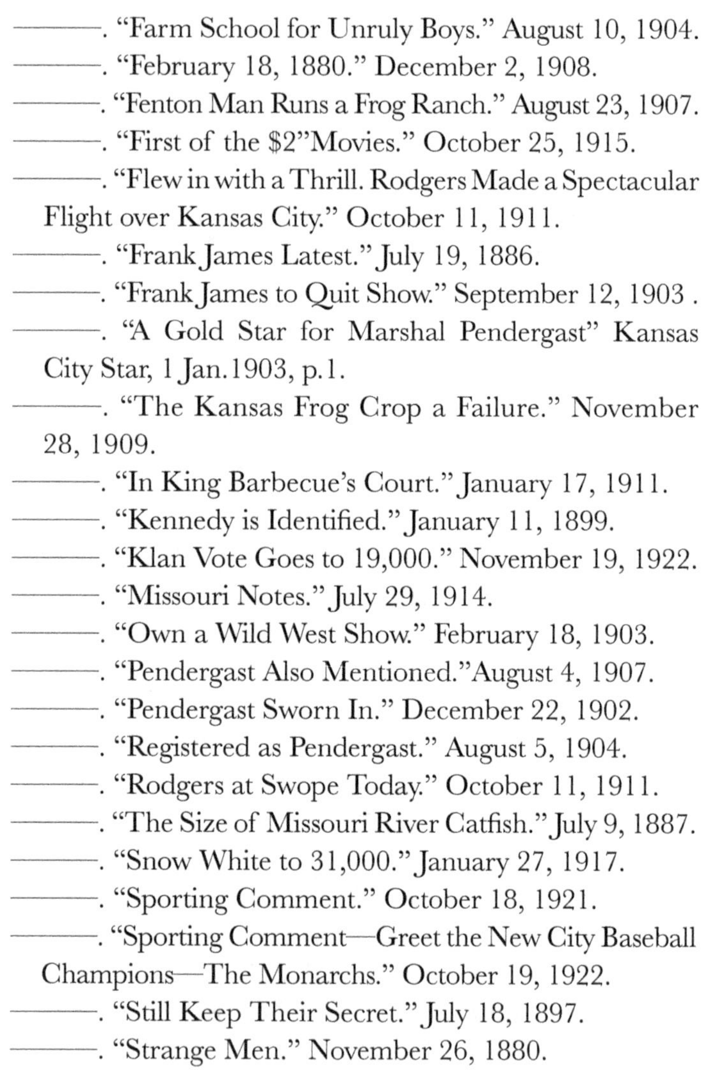

———. "Farm School for Unruly Boys." August 10, 1904.
———. "February 18, 1880." December 2, 1908.
———. "Fenton Man Runs a Frog Ranch." August 23, 1907.
———. "First of the $2"Movies." October 25, 1915.
———. "Flew in with a Thrill. Rodgers Made a Spectacular Flight over Kansas City." October 11, 1911.
———. "Frank James Latest." July 19, 1886.
———. "Frank James to Quit Show." September 12, 1903 .
———. "A Gold Star for Marshal Pendergast" Kansas City Star, 1 Jan.1903, p.1.
———. "The Kansas Frog Crop a Failure." November 28, 1909.
———. "In King Barbecue's Court." January 17, 1911.
———. "Kennedy is Identified." January 11, 1899.
———. "Klan Vote Goes to 19,000." November 19, 1922.
———. "Missouri Notes." July 29, 1914.
———. "Own a Wild West Show." February 18, 1903.
———. "Pendergast Also Mentioned."August 4, 1907.
———. "Pendergast Sworn In." December 22, 1902.
———. "Registered as Pendergast." August 5, 1904.
———. "Rodgers at Swope Today." October 11, 1911.
———. "The Size of Missouri River Catfish." July 9, 1887.
———. "Snow White to 31,000." January 27, 1917.
———. "Sporting Comment." October 18, 1921.
———. "Sporting Comment—Greet the New City Baseball Champions—The Monarchs." October 19, 1922.
———. "Still Keep Their Secret." July 18, 1897.
———. "Strange Men." November 26, 1880.

———. "They Came in Thousands." January 28, 1917.

———. "Thousands Went to Swope." October 11, 1911.

———. "To Start Kansas Frog Farm." April 6, 1907.

———. "Wanted: Homes" January 6, 1882.

———. "Wild West Show Starts." May 8, 1903.

———. "Will Go With Cole Younger"." April 18, 1903.

———. "Younger Suits Settled." October 13, 1903.

Kansas City Times. "A Streetcar "Palace' is Vacant" Kansas City Times, 5 Dec.1919 p. 12.

Liberty [Missouri] *Tribune.* "Grasshoppers by the Bushel." May 28, 1875.

JOURNALS

Duble, Charlie. "P.T. Barnum's Famous Jumbo." *Bandwagon* 1 (January–February 1856): 5–6.

Jones, Lila Lee. "The Ku Klux Klan in Eastern Kansas During the 1920s." *Emporia State Research Studies* 23 (Winter 1975): 3.

"Untitled." *Real McCoy, Neighborhood Council No. 15* 36, no. 6 (June 2006).

"Untitled." *Scientific American* (July 12, 1873): 17.

"Untitled." *St. Louis Herpetological Society Newsletter* 24, no. 1 (January 1997).

Ward, Stephanie Francis. "The Lawyer Who Took On Jesse James...and Won." *ABA Journal* (March 2008).

INTERNET

Frederickson, Alexandra. "The Chemistry of Film: The Exploding Entertainment Medium." http://www.voices/yahoo.com.

Friend, Harold. "MLB: Babe Ruth and Judge Landis Expressed Contempt for Baseball Fans." http://www.bleacherreport.com Aug. 13, 2011.

"Henry Perry-Father of Kansas City Barbecue." http://ocbarbecue.blogspot.com/2012/05/henry-perry-father-of-kansas-city.html.

Jackson, K.M. "Mickey and the Tramp: Walt Disney's Debt to Charlie Chaplin." *Journal of American Culture* 26. www.onlinelibrary.wiley.com/Doi:10.1111/1542-734X.00104/abstract.

Jenkinson, Bill. "Babe Ruth and the Issue of Race." http://www.baberuthcentral.com/the humanitarian/babe-ruth-and-the-issue-of-race-Bill-Jenkinson.

Llanos, Miguel. "Bloodhounds Used to Sniff Out People Killing Elephants for Ivory." http://www.worldnews.nbcnew.com/-2012/03/05/10582934-bloodhounds-used-to-sniff-out-people-killing-elephants-for-ivory?lite (.

Nadis, Steve. "SubTropolis U.S.A." *Atlantic* (May 2010). http://www.theatlantic.com/magazine/archive/2010/05/subtropolis-usa/8033.

O'Reilly, CuChullane. "Whisper on the Wind: The Tom Bass Story." *Horse Connection Magazine* 2008) (November and December). www.horseconnection.com/site/story-nov8.html.

"When the Skies Turned to Black: The Locust Plague of 1875." *Hearthstone Legacy Publications.* www.hearthstonelegacy.com/when-the-skies-turned-to-black-the_locust-plague-of-1875.htm.

www.guinnessworldrecords.com/world-records/3000/largest-attendance-at-a-film-screening.

www.lostpetdetection.com.

www.wattshaysletters.com/fam-stories-1.html.

Wyandotte Daily News, August 2, 2012. wyandottedailynews.com.

About the Author

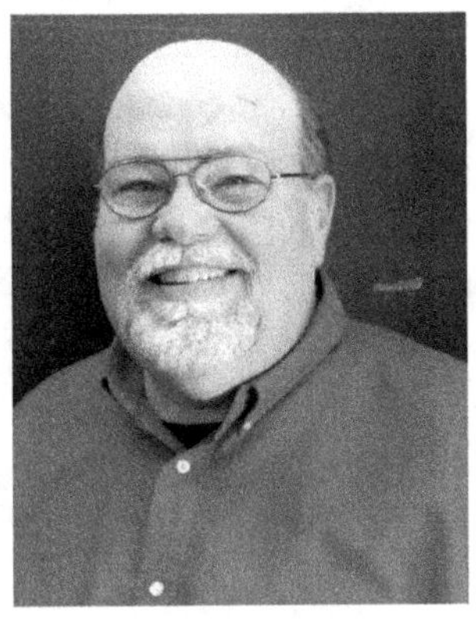

Paul Kirkman is the author of *The Battle of Westport: Missouri's Great Confederate Raid* (Charleston, SC: The History Press, 2011). He also co-authored *LOCKDOWN: Outlaws, Lawmen and Frontier Justice in Jackson County, Missouri* (Independence, MO: Jackson County Historical Society, 2009).

He has a BA in history from Columbia College (2005), and he completed an archival internship for the Jackson County, Missouri Historical Society, through which he gained the opportunity to work as a volunteer for the 1859 Marshal's Home and Jail Museum on the Historic Independence Square. Paul worked as an assistant archivist for the Kansas City Department of Parks, Recreation and Boulevards and is a past member of the State Historical Society of Missouri's Speakers' Bureau.

Mr. Kirkman continues to give presentations to groups with an interest in regional history, especially the border war and postwar outlaw era.

He has written articles, including "How to Discover Your Town's History: Research Tips and Resources for Local Historians" (*Yahoo Contributor Network*, September 17, 2010) and "Jackson County's Little Blue River Valley: Balancing Development and Preservation of an Historic Rural Landscape" (*Jackson County Missouri Historical Society Journal*, Autumn 2005) and is a member of the Westport Historical Society, the Jackson County Historical Society and the State Historical Society of Missouri.

Mr. Kirkman lives in Independence, Missouri, with his wife, Shawn, and daughter, Shannon.

www.ingramcontent.com/pod-product-compliance
Lightning Source LLC
La Vergne TN
LVHW010940100826
845153LV00002B/105

* 9 7 8 1 5 4 0 2 0 7 0 3 6 *